Engraved for Mrs Glasse's Complete art of Cookery.

THE COMPLETE
ART OF COOKERY,

EXHIBITED

IN A PLAIN AND EASY MANNER,

WITH

DIRECTIONS FOR MARKETING,

THE SEASON OF THE YEAR FOR

BUTCHERS' MEAT,
POULTRY, FISH, &c.

Embellished with Engravings,

SHEWING

THE ART OF TRUSSING, CARVING.

ETC. ETC. ETC.

BY

Mrs. GLASSE.

LONDON:

PUBLISHED BY H. QUELCH, 33, OLD 'CHANGE,
CHEAPSIDE, & 24, EAST STREET, WALWORTH.

1828.

Goose. *Pigeon.*

Turkey for Roasting.

Rabbits for Boiling.——Roasting

Fowl and Duck for Roasting.

CARVING.

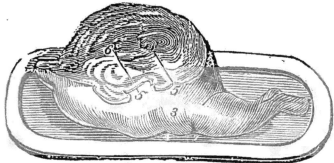

Leg of Mutton.

Roasted Pig.

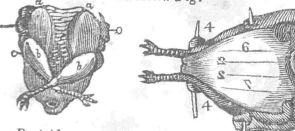

Partridge.   *Pheasant.*

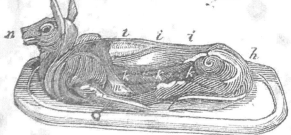

Hare.

THE COMPLETE
ART OF COOKERY.

I BELIEVE I have attempted a branch of Cookery which nobody has thought worth their while to write on, but as I have both seen, and found by experience, that the generality of servants are greatly wanting in that point, I have taken on me to instruct them in the best manner I am capable; and every servant that can read, will be capable of making a tolerable good cook; and those who have the least notion of cookery, cannot miss of being very good ones.

I do not pretend to teach professed cooks, my design being to instruct the ignorant and unlearned, (which will likewise be of use in all private families,) and that in so full and plain a manner, that the most ignorant person, who can but read, will know how to cook. As marketing mnst be the first branch of Cookery, I shall begin with that first.

DIRECTIONS HOW TO MARKET.

BUTCHERS' MEAT.

LAMB.

In a fore quarter of lamb mind the neck vein: if it be an azure blue, it is new and good; but if green or yellow, it is near tainting, if not tainted already. In the hinder quarter, smell under the kidney, and try the knuckle: if you meet with a faint scent, and the knuckle be limber, it is stale killed. For a lamb's head, mind the eyes: if sunk or wrinkled, it is stale; if plump and lively, it is

B 2

new and sweet. Lamb comes in in April, and holds
good till the end of August.

VEAL.

If the bloody vein in the shoulder looks blue, or
of a bright red it is new killed; but if black, green
or yellow, it is flabby and stale, if wrapped in wet
cloths, smell whether it be musty or not. For the
loin first taints under the kidney; and the flesh, if
stale killed, will be soft and slimy.

The breast and neck taints first at the upper end,
and you will perceive dusky, yellow, or green ap-
pearance; and the sweetbread on the breast will
be clammy, otherwise it is fresh and good. The
leg is known to be new by the stiffness of the joint:
if limber and the flesh seems clammy, and has green
or yellow specks, it is stale. The head is known
as the lamb's. The flesh of a bull-calf is more red
and firm than that of a cow-calf, and the fat more
hard curdled.

MUTTON.

If it be young, the flesh will pinch tender; if old,
it will wrinkle, and remain so: if young, the fat
will easily part from the lean; if old, it will stick
by strings and skins; if ram mutton, the fat feels
spongy, the flesh close grained and tough, not
rising again when dented: if ewe-mutton, the flesh
is paler than wether-mutton, a closer grain and
easily parting. If there be a rot, the flesh will be
pale, and the fat a faint white inclining to yellow,
and the flesh will be loose at the bone. If you
squeeze it hard, some drops of water will stand up
like sweat. As to the newness and staleness, the
same is to be observed as in lamb.

BEEF.

If it be right ox-beef, it will have an open grain; if young, a tender and oily smoothness; if rough and spongy, it is old, or inclined to be so, except the neck, brisket, and such parts as are very fibrous, which in young meat will be more rough than in other parts. A carnation, pleasant color, betokens good spending meat: the suet, a curious white; yellow is not good.

Cow-beef is less bound and closer grained than ox, the fat whiter, but the lean somewhat paler; if young, the dent made with the finger will rise again in a little time.

Bull-beef is close-grained, deep dusky red, tough in pinching, the fat skinny, hard, and has a rammish rank smell; and for newness, and staleness, this flesh bought fresh has but few signs, the more material is its clamminess, and the rest your smell will inform you. If it be bruised, these places will look more dusky or blacker than the rest.

PORK.

If young, the lean will break in pinching between the fingers; and if you nip the skin with your nails, it will make a dent; also if the fat be soft and pulpy, like lard: if the lean be tough, and the fat flabby and spongy, feeling rough, it is old, especially if the rind be stubborn, and you cannot nip it with your nails.

If a boar, though young, or a hog gelded at full growth, the flesh will be hard, tough, red, and rammish of smell; the fat skinny and hard; the skin thick and rough, and pinched up, will immediately fall again.

B 3

As for old or new killed, try the legs, hands, and springs, by putting the finger under the bone that comes out; if it be tainted, you will there find it by smelling the finger; besides the skin will be sweaty and clammy when stale, but cool and smooth when new.

If you find little kernels in the fat of the pork, like hail-shot, it is measly, and dangerous to be eaten. Pork comes in in the middle of August, and holds good till Lady-day.

How to choose Brawn, Venison, Westphalia Hams, &c.

Brawn is known to be old or young by the extraordinary or moderate thickness of the rind; the thick is old, the moderate young. If the rind and fat be tender, it is not boar brawn, but barrow or sow.

VENISON.

Try the haunches or shoulders under the bones that come out with your finger or knife, and as the scent is sweet or rank, it is new or stale; and the like of the sides in the fleshy parts; if tainted, they will look green in some places, or more than ordinary black. Look on the hoofs, and if the clefts are very wide and rough, it is old; if close and smooth it is young.

The buck venison begins in May, and is in high season till Allhallow's-day: the doe from Michaelmas to the end of December, or sometimes to the end of January.

WESTPHALIA HAMS AND ENGLISH BACON.

Put a knife under the bone that sticks out of the ham, and if it comes out in a manner clean, and has a curious flavour, it is sweet; if much smeered and dulled, it is tainted or rusty.

English gammons are tried the same way; and for other parts, try the fat; if it be white, oily in feeling, does not break or crumb it is good; but if the contrary, and the lean has little streaks of yellow, it is rusty, or will soon be so.

BUTTER, CHEESE, AND EGGS.

When you buy butter, trust not to that which will be given you, but try in the middle, and if your smell and taste be good, you cannot be deceived.

Cheese is to be chosen by its moist and smooth coat; if old cheese be rough coated, rugged, or dry at top, beware of little worms or mites: if it be over full of holes, moist or spongy, it is subject to maggots; if soft or perished places appear on the outside, try how deep it goes, the greater part may be hid.

Eggs, hold the great end to your tongue; if it feels warm it is new; if cold bad; and so in proportion to the heat or cold, is the goodness of the egg. Another way to know, is to put the egg in a pan of cold water, the fresher the egg, the sooner it will fall to the bottom; if rotten, it will swim at the top. This is a sure way not to be deceived. As to the keeping of them, pitch them all with the small end downwards in fine wood ashes, turning them once a week endways, and they will keep some months,

POULTRY IN SEASON.

January.— Hen turkeys, capons, pullets with eggs, fowls, chickens, hares, all sorts of wild fowl, tame rabbits, and tame pigeons.

February. — Turkeys, and pullets with eggs, capons, fowls, small chickens, hares, all sorts of wild-fowl, (which in this month begins to decline,) tame and wild pigeons, tame rabbits, green geese, young ducklings, and turkey poults.

March.—This month the same as the preceding; and in this month wild-fowl goes quite out.

April.—Pullets, spring fowls, chickens, pigeons, young wild rabbits, leverets, young geese, ducklings, and turkey poults.

May and June.—The same.

July.- ·The same; with young partridges, pheasents, and wild ducks, called flappers or moolters.

August.—The same.

September, October, November, and December. —In these months all sorts of fowl, both wild and tame, are in season; and in the three last is the full season for all wild fowl.

HOW TO CHOOSE POULTRY.
To know if a Capon is a true one, young or old new or stale.

If it be young, his spurs are short, and his legs, smooth : if a true capon, a fat vein on the side of his breast, the comb pale, and a thick belly and rump: if new, he will have a hard close vent; if stale, a loose open vent.

A COCK OR HEN TURKEY, TURKEY POULTS.

If the cock be young, his legs will be black and smooth, and his spurs short: if stale, his eyes will be sunk in his head, and the feet dry; if new, the eyes lively, and feet limber. Observe the like by the hens; and, moreover, if she be with egg, she will have a soft open vent; if not, a hard close vent. Turkey poults are known the same, their age cannot deceive you.

A COCK, HEN, &c.

If young, his spurs are short and dubbed; but take particular notice they are not pared or scraped: if old, he will have an open vent; but if new, a close hard vent. And so of a hen for newness or staleness; if old, her legs and comb are rough; if young, smooth.

A TAME, WILD, AND BRAN GOOSE.

If the bill be yellow, and she has but a few hairs, she is young; but if full of hairs, and the bill and foot red, she is old; if new, limber-footed; if stale, dry-footed. And so of a wild and bran goose.

WILD AND TAME DUCKS.

The duck, when fat, is hard and thick on the belly; if not, thin and lean; if new, limber-footed; if stale, dry-footed. A true wild duck has a red foot, smaller than the tame one.

PHEASANT, COCK AND HEN.

The cock, when young, has dubbed spurs; when old, sharp small spurs: if, new, a fat vent; if stale, an open flabby one. The hen, if young, has smooth legs, and her flesh of a curious grain; if with egg, she will have a soft open vent; if not, a close one. For newness or staleness, as the cock.

PARTRIDGE, COCK, AND HEN.

The bill white, and the legs blue, show age; for if young, the bill is black, and the legs yellow; if new, a fast vent; if stale, a green and open one. If full crops, and they have fed on green wheat, they may taint there; for this smell the mouth.

WOODCOCK, AND SNIPE.

The woodcock, if fat, is thick and hard, if new, limber-footed; when stale, dry-footed; or if their noses are snotty, and their throats muddy and moorish, they are not good. A snipe, if fat, has a fat vein on the side under the wing, and in the vent feels thick. For the rest, like the woodcock.

DOVES AND PIGEONS.

To know the turtle-dove, look for a blue ring round his neck, and the rest mostly white. The stock-dove is bigger; and the ring-dove is less than the stock-dove. The dove-house pigeons, when old, are red-legged; if new and fat, they will feel full and fat in the vent, and are limber-footed; but if stale, a flabby and green vent.

So the green or grey plover, fieldfare, blackbird, thrush, larks, &c.

OF HARE, LEVERET, OR RABBIT.

Hare will be white and stiff, if new and clean killed: if stale, the flesh black in most parts, and the body limber: if the cleft in her lips spread much, and her claws wide and ragged, she is old; the contrary young: if young, the ears will tear like brown paper; if old, dry and tough. To know a true leveret, feel on the fore-leg, near the foot, and if there is a small bone or knob, it is right: if not it is a hare; for the rest, observe as in a hare. A rabbit, if stale, will be limber and slimy; if new, white and stiff; if old, her claws are long and rough, the wool mottled with grey hairs; if young, claws and wool smooth.

FISH IN SEASON.

Candlemas Quarter.

Lobsters, crabs, craw-fish, river crawfish, guard-fish, mackarel, bream, barbel, roach, shad or alloc, lamprey or lamper-eels, dace, bleak, prawns, and horse-mackerel.

The eels that are taken in running water are better than pond eels; of these the silver ones are most esteemed.

Midsummer Quarter.

Turbot, trout, soals, grigs, shafflings and glout, tenes, salmon, dolphin, flying-fish, sheep-head, tollis, both land and sea, sturgeon, scale, chub, lobsters, and crabs.

Sturgeon is commonly found in the northern seas; but now and then we find them in our great rivers, the Thames, the Severn, and the Tyne. This fish is of a large size, and will sometimes measure eighteen feet in length. They are much esteemed when fresh, cut in pieces, roasted, baked, or pickled for cold treats. The caveer is esteemed a dainty, which is the spawn of this fish. The latter end of this quarter come smelts.

Michaelmas Quarter.

Cod, haddock, coal-fish, white and pouting hake, lyng, tuske, mullet, red and grey, weaver, gurnet, rocket, herring, sprats, soals, flounders, plaice, dabs, smeare-dabs, eels, chars, scate, thornback, homlyn, kinson, oysters, scollops, salmon, seaperch, and carp, pike, tench, and sea-tench.

Scate-maids are black, and thornback-maids white. Grey bass comes with the mullet.

In this quarter are fine smelt, and holds till after Christmas.

There are two sorts of mullets, the sea-mullet and the river-mullet, both equally good.

Christmas Quarter.

Dore, brill, gudgeons, gollin, smelts, crouch, perch, anchovy, loach, scollops, wilks, periwinkles, cockles, muscles, geare, bearbet, and hollebet.

HOW TO CHOOSE FISH.

To choose Salmon, Pike, Trent, Carp, Tench, Grailing, Barbel, Chub, Ruff, Eel, Whiting, Smelt, Shad, &c.

All these are known to be new or stale by the color of their gills, their easiness or hardness to open, the hanging or keeping up of the fins, the standing out or sinking of the eyes, and by smelling the gills.

TURBOT.

He is chosen by his thickness and plumpness: and if his belly be of a cream colour, he must spend well; but if thin, and his belly of a blueish white, he will eat very loose.

COD AND CODLING.

Choose by his thickness towards the head, and the whiteness of his flesh when it is cut; and so of a codling.

LYNG.

For dried ling, choose that which is thickest in the poll, and the flesh of the brightest yellow.

SCATE AND THORNBACK.

These are chosen by their thickness; and the she scate is the sweetest, especially if large,

SOALS.

These are chosen by their thickness and stiffness. When their bellies are of a cream color, they spend the firmer.

STURGEON.

If it cuts without crumbling, and the veins and gristles give a true blue where they appear, and the flesh a perfect white, then conclude it to be good.

FRESH HERRINGS AND MACKEREL.

If their gills are of a lively shining redness, their eyes stand full, and the fish is stiff, then they are new; but if dusky and faded, or sinking and wrinkled, and tails limber, they are stale.

LOBSTERS.

Choose by their weight; the heaviest are best. if no water be in them; if new, the tail will pull smart, like a spring ; if full, the middle of the tail will be full of hard, or red-skinned meat. A cock lobster is known by the narrow back part of the tail, and the two uppermost fins within the tail are stiff and hard ; but the hen is soft, and the back of her tail broader.

PRAWNS, SHRIMPS, AND CRAB-FISH.

The two first, if stale, will be limber, and cast a kind of slimy smell, their color fading, and they slimy : the latter will be limber in their claws and joints, their red color blackish and dusk, and will have an ill smell under their throats ; otherwise all of them are good.

PLAICE AND FLOUNDERS.

If they are stiff, and their eyes be not sunk or

look dull, they are new : the contrary when stale.
The best sort of plaice look blue on the belly.

PICKLED SALMON.

If the flesh feels oily, and the scales are stiff and
shining, and it comes in flakes, and parts without
crumbling, then it is new and good, and not otherwise.

PICKLED AND RED HERRINGS.

For the first, open the back to the bone, and if
the flesh be white, flaky, and oily, and the bone
white, or a bright red, they are good. If the latter
carry a good gloss, part well from the bone, and
smell well, then conclude them to be good.

OF ROASTING, BOILING, &c.

That professed cooks will find fault with my
touching on a branch of cookery which they never
thought worth their notice, is what I expect.
However, this I know, it is the most necessary part
of it; and few servants know how to roast and
boil to perfection.

I shall begin with roast and boiled of all sorts,
and the cook must order her fire according to what
she is to dress. If any thing little or thin, then
a brisk little fire, that it may be done quick and
nice ; if a very large joint, be sure a good fire be
laid to cake : let it be clear at the bottom ; and when
the meat is half done, move the dripping-pan and
spit a little from the fire, and stir up a brisk fire :
for according to the goodness of the fire, your
meat will be done soon or late.

BEEF.

Be sure to paper the top, and baste it well while
roasting, and throw a handful of salt on it. When

:you see the smoke draw to the fire, it is near
:enough: take off the paper, baste it well, aud
(drudge it with a little flour to make a fine froth.
Never salt roast meat before you lay it to the fire,
for it draws out the gravy. If you would keep it
a few days before you dress it, dry it with a cloth,
and hang it where the air will come to it; be sure
there is no damp place about it, When you take
up your meat, garnish the dish with horse-radish.

MUTTON AND LAMB.

As to roasting of mutton, the loin, haunch, and
saddle must be done as the beef above; but all
other sorts of mutton and lamb must be roasted
with a quick clear fire, and without paper; baste
it when you lay it down; and just before you take
it up, drudge it with a little flour; but be sure
not to use too much, for that takes away all the
fine taste of the meat. Some choose to skin a loin
of mutton, and roast it brown without paper; but
that you may do just as you please; but be sure
always to take the skin off a breast of mutton.

VEAL.

As to veal be careful to roast it of a fine brown:
if a large joint a good fire; if small, a little brisk
fire; if a fillet or loin, be sure to paper the fat,
that you loose as little of that as possible: lay it
some distance from the fire, till it is soaked, then
lay it near the fire. When you lay it down, baste
it well with good butter; and when it is near
enough, baste it again, and drudge it with a little
flour. The breast you must roast with the caul on
till it is enough, take off the caul, baste it, and
drudge it with a little flour.

PORK.

Pork must be well done, or it is apt to surfeit.
When you roast a loin, take a sharp penknife and
cut the skin across, to make the crackling eat the
better.   Cut the chine, and all pork that has the
rind on.   Roast a leg of pork thus: take a knife
and score it; stuff the knuckle part with sage and
onion, chopped fine with pepper and salt; or cut
a hole under the twist, and put the sage &c. there,
and skewer it up with a skewer.   Roast it crisp,
because most people like the rind crisp, which they
call crackling.   Make apple sauce, and send up in
a boat; then have a little drawn gravy to put in
the dish.   This they call a mock goose.   The
spring, or hand of pork, if young, roasted like a
pig, eats very well, otherwise it is better boiled.
The spare-rib should be basted with a bit of butter,
a little dust of flour, and some sage shred small;
but we never make any sauce to it but apple.   The
best way to dress pork griskins is to roast them,
baste them with a little butter and sage, and pepper
and salt.   Few eat any thing with these but
mustard.

TO ROAST A PIG.

Spit a pig, and lay it to the fire, which must be
a very good one at each end, or hang a flat iron
in the middle of the grate.   Before you lay the
pig down, take a little sage shred small, a piece of
butter as big as a walnut, and pepper and salt, put
them in the pig, and sew it up with coarse thread;
flour it well over, and keep flouring it till the eyes
drop out, or you find the crackling hard.   Be sure
to save all the gravy that comes out of it, which

you must do by setting basons or pans under the
pig in the dripping-pan, as soon as you find the
gravy begins to run. When the pig is enough,
stir the fire up brisk; take a coarse cloth, with
about a quarter of a pound of butter in it, and rub
the pig over till the crackling is crisp, then take it
up. Lay it in a dish, and with a sharp knife cut
off the head, then cut the pig in two, before you
draw out the spit. Cut the ears off the head, and
lay them at each end; cut the under jaw in two,
and lay on each side: melt some good butter, take
the gravy you saved, and put in it, boil it, and
pour it in the dish with the brains bruised fine,
and the sage mixed together, and then send it to
table.

Another Way to roast a Pig

Chop sage and onion very fine, a few crumbs of
bread, a little butter, pepper, and salt, rolled up
together; put it in the belly, and sew it up: before
you lay down the pig, rub it all over with sweet oil.
When done, take a dry cloth, and wipe it, then put
it in a dish, cut it up, and send it to table with the
sauce as above.

Different sorts of Sauce for a Pig.

You are to observe there are several ways of
making sauce for a pig. Some do not love sage,
only a crust of bread, but then you should have a
little dried sage rubbed and mixed with the gravy
and butter. Some love bread sauce in a bason,
made thus: take a pint of water, put in a good
piece of crumb of bread, a blade of mace, and a
little whole pepper; boil it about five or six minutes,
then pour the water off, take out the spice, and

beat up the bread with a good piece of butter. Some
love a few currants boiled in it, a glass of wine, and
a little sugar : but that you may do just as you
like.   Others take half a pint of beef gravy, and
the gravy which comes out of the pig, with a piece
of butter rolled in flour, two spoonfuls of catchup,
and boil them all together, then take the brains of
the pig and bruise them fine : put these with the
sage in the pig, and pour in the dish : it is a very
good sauce. When you have not gravy enough
come out of your pig with the butter for sauce, take
half a pint of veal gravy, and add to it ; or stew
pettytoes, and take as much of that liquor as will
do for sauce mixed with the other.

TO BAKE A PIG.

If you cannot roast a pig, lay it in in a dish, flour
it all over well and rub it over with butter ; butter
the dish you lay it in, and put it in the oven.
When it is enough, draw it out of the oven's mouth
and rub it over with a buttery cloth ; then put it in
the oven again till it is dry ; take it out and lay it
in a dish ; cut it up, take a little veal gravy ; and
take of the fat in the dish it was baked in, and
there will be some good gravy at the bottom ; put
that to it with a little piece of butter rolled in flour ;
boil it up, and put it in the dish with the brains and
sage in the belly.   Some love a pig brought whole
to table, then you are only to put what sauce you
like in the dish.

TO MELT BUTTER.

In melting butter you must be very careful : let
the saucepan be well tinned : take a spoonful of
water, a little dust of flour, and butter cut in pieces ;

be sure to keep shaking the pan one way, for fear it should oil: when melted, let it boil and it will be smooth and fine. A silver pan is best.

TO ROAST GEESE, TURKEYS, &c.

When you roast a goose, turkey, or fowl of any sort, singe them with a piece of white paper, and baste them with a piece of butter; drudge them with a little flour; and when the smoke begins to draw to the fire, and they look plump, baste them again, and drudge them with a little flour, and take them up.

SAUCE FOR A GOOSE.

For a goose make a little good gravy, and put it in a bason by itself, and some apple sauce in another.

SAUCE FOR A TURKEY.

For a turkey, good gravy in the dish, and bread or onion sauce in a bason.

SAUCE FOR FOWLS.

To fowls you should put good gravy in the dish, and either bread or egg sauce in a bason.

SAUCE FOR DUCKS.

For ducks a little gravy in the dish, an onion in a cup, if liked.

SAUCE FOR PHEASANTS AND PARTRIDGES.

Pheasants and partridges should have gravy in the dish, and bread sauce in a cup, and poverroy-sauce.

SAUCE FOR LARKS.

Roast larks, and all the time they are roasting, baste them very gently with butter, and sprinkle crumbs of bread on them till they are almost done; then let them brown before you take them up.

c

The best way of making crumbs of bread is to rub them through a fine cullender, and put a little butter in a stew pan : melt it, put in your crumbs of bread, and keep them stirring till they are of a light brown; put them in a sieve to drain a few minutes, lay your larks in a dish, and the crumbs all round, almost as high as the larks, with plain butter in a cup, and some gravy in another.

TO ROAST WOODCOCKS AND SNIPES.

Put them on a little spit; take a round of a threepenny loaf, and toast it brown, then lay it in a dish under the birds: baste them with a little butter, and let the trale drop on the toast.   When they are roasted, put the toast in the dish, lay the woodcocks on it, and have a quarter of a pint of gravy; pour it in a dish, and set it over a lamp or chafing dish for three minutes, and send them to table.

You are to observe, we never take any thing out of a woodcock or snipe.

TO ROAST A PIGEON.

Take some parsley shred fine, a piece of butter as big as a walnut, a little pepper and salt; tie the neck end tight; tie a string round the legs and rump, and fasten the other end to the top of the chimney-piece.   Baste with butter, and when they are enough lay them in a dish, and they will swim with gravy.   You may put them on a little spit, and tie both ends close.

TO BROIL A PIGEON.

When you broil them, do them in the same manner, and take care your fire is clear, and set your gridiron high, that they may not burn, and have a little parsley and butter in a cup.   You may split

..and broil them with a little pepper and salt; and
you may roast them only with parsley and butter in
a dish.

Directions for Geese and Ducks.

As to geese and ducks, you should have sage and
onion shred fine, with pepper and salt put into the
belly.

Put only pepper and salt in wild ducks, easter-
lings, wigeon, teal, and all other sorts of wild fowl,
with gravy in the dish.

TO ROAST A HARE.

Take a hare when it is cased, truss it in this
manner: bring the two hind-legs up to its sides,
pull the fore-legs back, put your skewer first into
the hind-leg, then in the fore-leg, and thrust it
through the body; put the fore-leg on, and then
the hind-leg, and a skewer through the top of the
shoulder and back part of the head, which will
hold the head up. Make a pudding thus: take a
quarter of a pound of beef-suet, as much crumb of
bread, a handful of parsley, chopped fine, sweet
herbs of all sorts, such as basil, marjorum, winter-
savory, and a little thyme, chopped very fine, a
little nutmeg grated, lemon-peel cut fine, pepper
and salt; chop the liver fine, and put it in with two
eggs, mix it and put it in the belly; sew or skewer
it up; spit it, and lay it to the fire, which must be
a good one.

Different sorts of Sauce for a Hare.

Take a pint of cream, and half a pound of fresh
butter; put them in a saucepan, and keep stirring
it with a spoon till the butter is melted, and the
sauce is thick; then take up the hare, and pour the

c 2

sauce in a dish. Another way to make sauce for a hare, is to make good gravy, thickened with a little butter rolled in flour, and pour it in the dish. You may leave the butter out if you do not like it, and have currant jelly warmed in a cup, or red wine and sugar boiled to a syrup, done thus—take half a pint of red wine, a quarter of a pound of sugar, and set over a slow fire to simmer for a quarter of an hour. You may do half the quantity, and put it in a sauce-boat or bason.

TO BROIL STEAKS.

First have a very clear brisk fire; let your gridiron be very clean; take a chafing-dish, with a few hot coals out of the fire. Put the dish on it which is to lay your steaks on; then take fine rump-steaks half an inch thick, put a little pepper and salt on them, lay them on the gridiron, and (if you like it) take a shalot or two, or a good onion, and cut it fine; put it in a dish. Do not turn your steaks till the one side is done; then when you turn the other side there will soon be a fine gravy lie on the top of the steak, which you must be careful not to lose. When the steaks are enough, take them carefully off into your dish, that none of the gravy be lost: have ready a hot dish and cover, and carry them hot to table.

Directions concerning the Sauce for Steaks.

If you have pickles or horse-radish with steaks, never garnish your dish, because the garnish will be dry and the steaks cold; lay these things on little plates, and carry to table. The great nicety is to have them hot and full of gravy.

General Directions concerning Broiling.

As to mutton and pork steaks, you must keep

them turning quick on the gridiron, and have your dish ready over a chafing-dish of hot coals, and carry them to table covered hot. When you broil fowls or pigeons, always take care your fire is clear; and never baste any thing on the gridiron, for it only makes it smoked and burnt.

General Directions concerning Boiling.

As to all sorts of boiled meats, allow a quarter of an hour to every pound : be sure the pot is very clean, and skim it well, for every thing will have a scum rise; and if it boils down, it makes the meat black. All sorts of fresh meat you are to put in when the water boils, but salt meat when the water is cold.

TO BOIL A HAM.

When you boil a ham put it in the copper whilst the water is cold; when it boils, be careful it boils slowly. A ham of twenty pounds takes four hours and a half, larger and smaller in proportion. Keep the copper well skimmed. A green ham wants no soaking; but an old ham must be soaked sixteen hours, in a large tub of soft water.

TO BOIL A TONGUE.

A tongue, if soft, put in a pot over night, and do not let it boil till about three hours before dinner, then boil all that three hours : if fresh out of the pickle, two hours and a half, and put it in when the water boils.

TO BOIL FOWLS AND HOUSE LAMB.

Fowls and house lamb boil in a pot by themselves, in a good deal of water; and if any scum arises, take it off. They will be sweeter and whiter than if boiled in a cloth. A little chicken will be done in fifteen minutes, a large one in twenty miñutes, a good fowl in half an hour, a little turkey or goose in an hour, and a large turkey in an hour and a half.

Sauce for a Boiled Turkey.

The best sauce for a boiled turkey is good oyster and celery sauce. Make oyster sauce thus: a pint of oysters, set them off, strain the liquor from them, put them in cold water, and wash and beard them: put them in your liquor, in a stewpan, with a blade of mace, and butter rolled in flour, and a quarter of a lemon; boil them up, then put in half a pint of cream, and boil it all gently; take the lemon and mace out, squeeze the juice of the lemon into the sauce, then serve it in the boats. Make celery sauce thus: take the white part of the celery, cut it about one inch long: boil it in some water till it is tender; then take half a pint of veal broth, a blade of mace, and thicken it with a little flour and butter; put in half a pint of cream, boil them up gently together, put in your celery, and boil it up; then pour it into your boats.

Sauce for a boiled Goose.

Sauce for a boiled goose must be either onions or cabbage, first boiled, and then stewed in butter for five minutes.

Sauce for boiled Ducks and Rabbits.

To boiled ducks or rabbits, you must pour boiled onions over them, done thus: take the onions, peel and boil them in a great deal of water, shift your water, then let them boil about two hours; take them up, and throw them in the cullender to drain; then with a knife chop them on a board; put them in a saucepan; shake a little flour over them, put in a little milk or cream, with a piece of butter; set them over the fire, and when the butter is melted they are enough. But if you want sauce in half an hour, take onions, peel and cut them in thin slices; put them in milk and water, and when the water boils they will be done in twenty minutes; then throw them in a cullender to drain, chop them and put them in a saucepan; shake in a little flour, with a little cream, and a bit of butter; stir all together over the fire till the butter is melted, and they will be very fine. This sauce is very good with roast mutton, and it is the best way of boiling onions.

TO ROAST VENISON.

Take a haunch of venison and spit it; well butter four sheets of paper, put two on the haunch; then make a paste with flour, butter, and water; roll it out half as big as the haunch, and put it over the fat part; then put the other two sheets of paper on and tie them with packthread; lay it to a brisk fire, and baste it well all the time of roasting. If a large haunch of twenty-four pounds, it will take three hours and a half, except it is a very large fire, then three hours will do: smaller in proportion.

TO DRESS A HAUNCH OF MUTTON.

Hang it up a fortnight, and dress it as directed for a haunch of venison.

Different sorts of Sauce for Venison.

Take either of these sauces for Venison: currant jelly warmed, or half a pint of red wine, with a quarter of a pound of sugar, simmered over a clear fire for five or six minutes; or half a pint of vinegar, and a quarter of a pound of sugar, simmered to syrup.

TO ROAST MUTTON VENISON-FASHION.

Take a hind quarter of fat mutton, and cut the leg like a haunch; lay it in a pan with the back-side of it down; pour a bottle of red wine over it, and let it lie twenty-four hours : spit it and baste it with the same liquor and butter all the time it is roasting at a. quick fire, and an hour and a half will do it. Have a good gravy in a cup, and sweet sauce in another. A good fat neck of mutton eats finely done thus.

To keep Venison or Hare sweet, or to make them fresh when they stink.

If venison be very sweet, only dry it with a cloth, and hang it where the air comes. If you would keep it any time, dry it well with clean cloths, rub it all over with beaten ginger, and hang it in an airy place, and it will keep a great while. If it stinks or is musty, take lukewarm water, and wash it clean; then fresh milk and water lukewarm, and wash it again; then dry it in clean cloths very well, and rub it all over with beaten ginger, and hang it in an airy place. When you roast it, you need only wipe it with a clean cloth, and paper it as before-mentioned. Never do any thing else to venison, for all other things spoil your venison, and take away the fine flavour, and this preserves it better than any thing you can do. A hare you may manage just the same way.

TO ROAST A TONGUE OR UDDER.

Parboil it first, then roast it. stick eight or ten cloves about it, baste it with butter, and have gravy and sweet sauce. An udder eats very well done the same way.

TO ROAST RABBITS.

Baste them with good butter, and drudge them with a little flour. Half an hour will do them at a very quick clear fire; and if they are small, twenty minutes will do them. Take the liver, with a little bunch of parsley, and boil them, and then chop them very fine together. Melt some butter, and put half the liver and parsley into the butter; pour it in the dish, and garnish the dish with the other half. Let your rabbits be done of a fine light brown.

TO ROAST A RABBIT HARE-FASHION.

Lard a rabbit with bacon; roast it as you do a hare, and it eats very well; but you must make gravy sauce; but if you do not lard it, white sauce.

TURKEYS, PHEASANTS, &c. may be larded.

You may lard a turkey or pheasant, or any thing, just as you like it.

TO ROAST A FOWL PHEASANT-FASHION.

If you should have but one pheasant, and want two in a dish, take a full grown fowl, keep the head on, and truss it just as you do a pheasant; lard it with bacon, but do not lard the pheasant, and nobody will know it.

Rules to be observed in Roasting.

In the first place take care the spit be very clean, and be sure to clean it with nothing but sand and water. Wash it clean, and wipe it with a dry cloth; for oil, brick-dust, &c. will spoil your meat.

BEEF.

To roast a piece of beef of ten pounds, will take an hour and a half, at a good fire. Twenty pounds

weight will take three hours, if it be a thick piece;
but if a thin piece of twenty pounds weight, two
hours and a half will do it; and so on, according
to the weight of your meat, more or less.   Observe,
in frosty weather your beef will take half an hour
longer.

MUTTON.

A leg of mutton of six pounds will take an hour
at a quick fire; if frosty weather, an hour and a
quarter : nine pounds an hour and a half : a leg
of twelve pounds will take two hours; if frosty,
two hours and a half.   A large saddle of mutton
three hours, because of papering it; a small saddle
will take an hour and a half; and so on, according
to the size : a breast half an hour, at a quick fire;
a neck, if large, an hour; if very small better than
half an hour : a shoulder much the same time as a leg.

PORK.

Pork must be well done.   To every pound allow
a quarter of an hour: for example, a joint of twelve
pounds weight, three hours, and so on.   If it be a
thin piece of that weight, two hours will roast it.

Directions concerning Beef, Mutton, and Pork.

These three you may baste with fine nice dripping.   Be sure your fire be very good and brisk,
but do not lay your meat too near, for fear of
burning or scorching.

VEAL.

Veal takes much the same time roasting as
pork; but be sure to paper the fat of a loin or
fillet, and baste your veal with good butter.

HOUSE-LAMB.

If a large fore-quarter, an hour and a half; if a
small one, an hour.   The outside must be papered,

basted with good butter, and you must have a very quick fire. If a leg, three quarters of an hour; a neck, a breast, or shoulder, three quarters of an hour; if very small, half an hour will do.

A PIG.

If just killed, an hour; if killed the day before, an hour and a quarter: if a very large one, an hour and a half. But the best way to judge, is when the eyes drop out, and the skin is grown very hard; then rub it with a coarse cloth, with a good piece of butter rolled in it, till the crackling is crisp, and of a fine light brown.

A HARE.

You must have a quick fire. If it be a small hare, put three pints of milk and half a pound of fresh butter in the dripping-pan, which must be very clean: if a large one, two quarts of milk, and half a pound of fresh butter. You must baste it well with this all the time it is roasting; and when the hare has soaked up all the butter and milk it will be enough.

A TURKEY AND GOOSE.

A middling turkey will take an hour; a very large one, an hour and a quarter; a small one, three quarters of an hour. You must paper the breast till it is near done enough; take the paper off and froth it up. Your fire must be good.

FOWLS AND DUCKS.

A large fowl, three quarters of an hour; a middling one, half an hour; very small chickens, twenty minutes. Your fire must be quick and clear when you lay them down.

WILD DUCKS, TEAL, &c.

Twenty minutes. If you love them well done, twenty-five minutes.

PIGEONS AND LARKS.

Twenty minutes.

Directions concerning Poultry.

If your fire is not very quick and clear when you lay your poultry down to roast, it will not eat near so sweet, nor look so beautiful to the eye.

To keep Meat Hot.

The best way to keep meat hot, if done before company is ready, is to set the dish over a pan of boiling water; cover the dish with a deep cover so as not to touch the meat, and throw a cloth over all. Thus you may keep meat hot a long time, and it is better than over-roasting and spoiling it. The steam of the water keeps it hot, and does not draw the gravy out; whereas, if you set a dish of meat any time over a chafing-dish of coals, it will dry up all the gravy, and spoil the meat.

TO DRESS GREENS, ROOTS, &c.

Always be careful that your greens be nicely picked and washed. You should lay them in a clean pan for fear of sand or dust, which is apt to hang round wooden vessels. Boil all greens in a copper saucepan by themselves, with a great deal of water. Boil no meat with them, for that discolors them. Use no iron pans, &c. for they are not proper; only copper, brass, or silver.

SPINACH.

Pick it clean, and wash it in five or six waters; put it in a saucepan that will just hold it, throw over a little salt, and cover the pan close. Do not put any water in, but shake the pan often. Put your saucepan on a clear fire. As soon as you find the greens are shrunk and fallen to the bottom, and that the liquor which comes out boils up, they are enough. Throw them into a clean sieve to drain, and give them a little squeeze. Lay them in a plate, and never put any butter on it, but put it in a cup.

CABBAGES, &C.

Cabbage, and all sorts of young sprouts, must be boiled in a great deal of water. When the stalks are tender, or fall to the bottom, they are enough: then take them off, before they lose their colour. Always throw salt in your water before you put greens in. Young sprouts you send to table just as they are; but cabbage is best chopped, and put in a saucepan with a good piece of butter, stirring it for five or six minutes, till the butter is all melted, and then send it to table.

CARROTS.

Let them be scraped clean; and when they are enough, rub them in a clean cloth, then slice them into a plate, and pour some melted butter over them. If they are young spring carrots, half an hour will boil them. if large, an hour; but old Sandwich carrots will take two hours.

TURNIPS.

They eat best boiled in the pot; when enough, take them out, and put them in a pan, mash them with butter and a little salt, and send them to table. But you may do them thus: pare turnips, and cut them into dice, as big as the top of one's finger; put them into a clean saucepan, and cover

them with water. When enough, throw them in
a seive to drain, and put them in a saucepan with
a good piece of butter; stir them over the fire five
or six minutes, and send them to table.

PARSNIPS.

They should be boiled in a great deal of water;
and when they are soft, (which you will know by
running a fork into them,) take them up, and carefully scrape the dirt off them, and then with a knife
scrape them fine, throwing away all the sticky parts.
and send them up in a dish with melted butter.

BROCOLI.

Strip all the little branches off till you come to
the top one; then with a knife peel off the hard
outside skin, which is on the stalks and little
branches, and throw them in water, Have a stewpan of water with salt in it; when it boils, put in
the brocoli; and when the stalks are tender it is
enough : then send it to table, with a piece of toasted bread, soaked in the water it is boiled in, under
it, the same way as asparagus, with butter in a cup.
The French eat oil and vinegar with it.

POTATOES.

You must boil them in as little water as you
can, without burning the saucepan. Cover close
and when the skin begins to crack they are
enough. Drain all the water out, and let them
stand covered for a minute or two: then peel them,
lay them in a plate, and pour melted butter over
them. The best way to do them is, when they are
peeled, to lay them on a gridiron till they are of a
fine brown, and send them to table. Another way
is to put them in a saucepan with some good beef

dripping, cover them close, and shake the saucepan often, for fear of burning to the bottom. When they are of a fine brown, and crisp, take them up in a plate, then put them into another for fear of the fat, and put butter in a boat.

CAULIFLOWERS.

Cut the cauliflower-stalks off, leave a little green on, and boil them in spring water and salt: about fifteen minutes will do them. Take them out and drain them; send them whole in a dish, with some melted butter in a cup.

FRENCH BEANS.

First string them, then cut them in two, and again cross; but if you would do them nice, cut the bean in four, and then across, which is eight pieces. Lay them in water and salt; and when your pan boils, put in some salt and the beans. When they are tender, they are enough. Take care they do not lose their fine green. Lay them in a plate, and have butter in a cup.

ARTICHOKES.

Wring off the stalks, and put them in the water cold, with the tops downwards, that all the dust and sand may boil out. When the water boils, an hour and a half will do them.

ASPARAGUS.

Scrape all the stalks very carefully till they look white, then cut the stalks even alike, throw them in water, and have ready a stewpan boiling. Put in some salt, and tie the asparagus in little bundles. Let the water keep boiling, and when they are a little tender take them up. If you boil them too much, you lose both colour and taste. Cut the round of a small loaf, about half an inch thick, toast it brown on both sides, dip it in the asparagus liquor, and lay it in your dish: pour a little butter over the toast, then lay the asparagus on it all round the dish, with the white tops outward. Do not pour butter over the asparagus, for that makes it greasy to the fingers, but have butter in a bason, and send it to table.

Directions concerning Garden Things.

Most people spoil garden things by overboiling them. All things that are green should have a little crispiness; for if they are over boiled, they neither have any sweetness or beauty.

BEANS AND BACON.

When you dress beans and bacon, boil them separate, for the bacon will spoil the color of the beans. Always throw some salt in the water, and some parsley nicely picked. When the beans are enough, which you will know by their being tender, throw them into a cullender to drain. Take up the bacon, and skin it, throw some raspings of bread over the top; and if you have an iron, make it red hot, and hold it over to brown the top of the bacon; if you have not one, set it before the fire to brown. Lay the beans in the dish, and the bacon in the middle on the top, and send them to table, with parsley and butter in a bason,

To make Gravy for a Turkey, or any Sort of Fowls.

Take a pound of the lean part of beef, hack it with a knife, flour it well; have ready a stew-pan with a piece of fresh butter. When the butter is melted, put in the beef, fry it brown, and pour in a little boiling water, shake it round, and fill up with a tea-kettle of boiling water. Stir it all together and put in two or three blades of mace, four or five cloves, some whole pepper, an onion, a bundle of sweet herbs, a crust of bread, baked brown, and a little piece of carrot. Cover close, and let it stew till it is as good as you would have it. This will make a pint of rich gravy.

To make Veal, Mutton, and Beef Gravy.

Take a rasher or two of bacon or ham, lay it at the bottom of a stew-pan; put your meat, cut in thin slices, over it; then cut onions, turnips, carrots, and celery, a little thyme, and put over the meat, with a little allspice; put a little water at the bottom, set it on the fire, which must be a gentle one, and draw it till it is brown at the bottom, which you may know by the pan's hissing; then pour boiling water over it, and stew it gently for an hour and a half; if a small quantity, less time will do it. Season it with salt.

To burn Butter for thickening of Sauce.

Set butter on the fire, and let it boil till it is brown; then shake in some flour, and stir it all the time it is on the fire till it is thick. Put it by, and keep it for use. A little piece is what the cooks use to thicken and brown sauce; but there are few stomachs it agrees with, therefore seldom make use of it.

To make Gravy.

If you live in the country, where you cannot always have gravy meat, when meat comes from the butcher's, take a piece of beef, veal, and mutton; cut them into as small pieces as you can, and take a large deep saucepan with a cover, lay the beef at the bottom, then the mutton, then a very little piece of bacon, a slice or two of carrot, some mace, cloves, whole pepper, black and white, a large onion cut in slices, a bundle of sweet herbs, and then lay in the veal. Cover it close over a slow fire for six or seven minutes, shaking it now and then; then shake some flour in, and have ready some boiling water; pour it in till you cover the meat, and something more. Cover it close, and let it stew till it is rich and good: then season it to your taste with salt, and strain it off. This will suit most things.

TO BAKE A LEG OF BEEF.

Do it in the same manner as before directed in making gravy for soups, &c. And when it is baked, strain it through a coarse sieve. Pick out all the sinews and fat, put them in a saucepan with a few spoonfuls of the gravy, a little red wine, a little piece of butter rolled in flour, and some mustard: shake your saucepan often; and when the sauce is hot and thick, dish it up, and send it to table. It is a pretty dish.

TO BAKE AN OX'S HEAD.

Do it in the same manner as the leg of beef is directed to be done in making the gravy for soups, &c. and it does full as well for the same uses. If it should be too strong for any thing you want it put hot water to it. Cold water will spoil it.

PICKLED PORK.

Be sure you put it in when the water boils. If a middling piece, an hour will boil it; if a very large piece, an hour and a half, or two hours. If you boil it too long, it will go to jelly.

TO DRESS FISH.

Observe always in the frying of any sort of fish, first, that you dry it well in a clean cloth, then do your fish in this manner: beat up the yolks of two or three eggs, according to the quantity of fish, take a small pastry brush, and put the egg on, shake crumbs of bread and flour mixt over the fish and fry it. Let the stewpan you fry fish in be very nice and clean, and put in as much beef dripping, or hog's lard, as will almost cover the fish ; and be sure it boils before you put it in... Let it fry quick, and let it be of a fine light brown, but not too dark a colour. Have your fish-slice ready, and if there is occasion, turn it: when it is enough, take it up, and lay a coarse cloth on a dish, on which lay your fish, to drain all the grease from it. If you fry parsley, do it quick, and take great care to whip it out of the pan as soon as it is crisp, or it will lose its fine color. Take great care that your dripping be very nice and clean.

Some love fish in batter ; then you must beat an egg fine, and dip your fish in just as you are going to put it in the pan ; or as good a batter as any, is a little ale and flour beat up, just as you are ready for it, and dip the fish, to fry it.

LOBSTER SAUCE.

Take a fine hen lobster, take out all the spawn, and bruise it in a mortar very fine, with a little butter : take all the meat out of the claws and tail, and cut it in small square pieces ; put the spawn and meat in a stewpan, with a spoonful of anchovy-liquor and a spoonful of catchup, a blade of mace, a piece of a stick of horse-radish, half a lemon,

D

a gill of gravy, a little butter rolled in flour, just enough to thicken it; put in half a pound of butter nicely melted, boil it gently up for six or seven minutes; take out the horse-radish, mace, and lemon, and squeeze the juice of the lemon in the sauce; just simmer it up, and then put it in your boats.

SHRIMP SAUCE.

Take half a pint of shrimps, wash them very clean, put them in a stewpan with a spoonful of fish-lear, or anchovy-liquor, a pound of butter melted thick, boil it up for five minutes, and squeeze in half a lemon; toss it up, and put it in your cups or boats.

ANCHOVY SAUCE.

Take a pint of gravy, put in an anchovy, take a quarter of a pound of butter rolled in a little flour, and stir altogether till it boils. You may add a little juice of a lemon, catchup, red wine, and walnut liquor, just as you please.

Plain butter melted thick, with a spoonful of walnut pickle, or catchup, is a good sauce, or anchovy. In short, you may put as many things as you fancy in sauce.

TO DRESS A BRACE OF CARP.

Take a piece of butter, and put in a stewpan, melt it, and put in a large spoonful of flour, keep it stirring till it is smooth; then put in a pint of gravy, and a pint of red port or claret, a little horse-radish scraped, eight cloves, four blades of mace, and a dozen corns of allspice, tie them in a linen rag, a bundle of sweet herbs, half a lemon, three anchovies, a little onion chopped fine; season with pepper, salt, and cayenne, to your liking; stew it for half an hour, then strain it through a sieve into the pan you intend to put the fish in. Let the carp be well cleaned and scaled, put them in with the sauce, and stew them gently for half an hour; then turn them, and stew them fifteen minutes longer; put in with your fish some truffles and morels scalded, pickled mushrooms, an artichoke-bottom, and about a dozen large oysters, squeeze in the juice of half a lemon, stew it five minutes; then put the carp in a dish, and pour all the sauce over. Garnish with fried sippets, and the roe of the fish, done thus: beat the roe up well with the yolks of two eggs, a little flour, a little lemon-peel, chopped fine, pepper, salt, and a little anchovy-liquor; have ready a pan of beef-dripping boiling, drop the roe in, to be about as big as a crown-piece; fry it of a light brown, and put it round the dish with oysters fried in batter, and scraped horse-radish.

N.B. Stick your fried sippets in the fish.

You may fry the carp first, if you please, but the above is the most modern way. If you are in a great hurry, while the sauce is making, you may boil the fish in spring water, half a pint of vinegar, a little horse-radish, and bay leaf; put the fish in a dish, and pour the sauce over.

TO FRY CARP.

First scale and gut them, wash them clean, lay them in a cloth to dry, flour and fry them of a light brown. Fry toast, cut three-corner-ways, and the roes; when the fish is done, lay them on a coarse cloth to drain. Let the sauce be butter and anchovies, with the juice of lemon. Lay the carp in the dish, the roes on each side, and garnish them with fried toast and lemon.

TENCH.

Tench may be dressed the same way as carp.

TO BOIL A COD'S HEAD.

Set a fish-kettle on the fire, with water enough to boil it, a good handful of salt, a pint of vinegar, a bundle of sweet herbs, and a piece of horse-radish: let it boil a quarter of an hour, then put in the head, and when you are sure it is enough, lift up the fish-plate with the fish on it, set it across the kettle to drain, lay it in a dish, with the liver on one side. Garnish them with lemon and horse-radish scraped; melt butter, with a little of the fish liquor, an anchovy, oysters or shrimps, or what you fancy.

TO STEW COD.

Cut cod in slices an inch thick, lay them in the bottom of a large stewpan; season with nutmeg, beaten pepper, and salt, a bundle of sweet herbs, an onion, half a pint of white wine, and a quarter of a pint of water; cover close, and let it simmer softly for five or six minutes, then squeeze in the juice of a lemon, put in a few oysters and the liquor strained, a piece of butter as big as an egg, rolled in flour, and a blade or two of mace; cover close, and let it stew softly, shaking the pan often. When it is enough, take out the sweet herbs and onion, dish it up; pour the sauce over, and garnish with lemon.

TO BAKE COD'S HEAD.

Butter the pan you intend to bake it in, make

the head very clean, lay it in the pan, put in a bundle of sweet herbs, an onion stuck with cloves, three or four blades of mace, half a large spoonful of black and white pepper, a nutmeg bruised, a quart of water, a little piece of lemon-peel, and a little piece of horse-radish. Flour the head, grate a little nutmeg over it, stick pieces of butter all over it, and throw raspings all over that. Send it to the oven; when it is enough, take it out of that dish, and lay it carefully in the dish you intend to serve it up in. Set the dish over boiling water, and cover it up to keep it hot. In the mean time be quick, pour all the liquor out of the dish it was baked in into a saucepan, set it on the fire to boil three or four minutes, then strain it, and put to it a gill of red wine, two spoonfuls of catchup, a pint of shrimps, half a pint of oysters or muscels, liquor and all, but first strain it, a spoonful of mushroom pickle, a quarter of a pound of butter rolled in flour, stir it together till it is thick and boils; pour it in the dish, have ready toast cut three-corner-ways, and fried crisp. Stick pieces about the head and mouth, and lay the rest round the head. Garnish with lemon, notched, horse-radish, and parsley crisped in a plate before the fire. Lay one slice of lemon on the head, and serve it up hot.

To broil Crimp Cod, Salmon, Whiting, or Haddock.

Flour it, and have a quick clear fire, set the gridiron high, broil it of a fine brown, lay it in a dish, and for sauce have good melted butter. Take a lobster, bruise the spawn in the butter, cut the meat small, put altogether in the melted butter, make it hot, and pour it into your dish, or into basons. Garnish with horse-radish and lemon.

Oyster Sauce is made thus.

Take half a pint of oysters and simmer them till they are plump, strain the liquor from them through a sieve, wash the oysters clean, and beard them; put them in a stewpan, and pour the liquor over, but mind you do not pour the sediment with the liquor; add a blade of mace, a quarter of a lemon, a spoonful of anchovy-liquor, and a little bit of horse-radish, a little butter rolled in flour, half a pound of butter melted, boil it up gently for ten minutes; take out the horse-radish, the mace and lemon, squeeze the juice of the lemon in the sauce, toss it up a little, then put it into your boats or basons.

TO DRESS LITTLE FISH.

As to all sorts of little fish, such as smelts, roach, &c. they should be fried dry, and of a fine brown, and nothing but plain butter. Garnish with lemon.

And to boil salmon, the same, only garnish with lemon and horse-radish.

And with all boiled fish, you should put a good deal of salt and horse-radish in the water, except mackerel, with which put salt and mint, parsley and fennel, which chop to put in the butter; some love scalded gooseberries with them. Be sure to boil your fish well; but take great care they do not break.

TO BROIL MACKEREL.

Clean them, split them down the back, season with pepper and salt, mint, parsley, and fennel, chopped fine, and flour them: broil of a light brown, put them on a dish and strainer. Garnish with parsley; sauce, fennel and butter in a boat.

TO BOIL A TURBOT.

Lay it in a good deal of salt and water an hour or two, and if it is not quite sweet, shift the water five or six times; first put a good deal of salt in the mouth and belly.

In the mean time set on a fish kettle with spring water and salt, a little vinegar, and a piece of horse-radish. When the water boils, lay the turbot on a fish-plate, put it in the kettle, let it be well boiled, but take great care it is not too much done; when enough, take off the fish-kettle, set it before the fire, then carefully lift up the fish plate, and set it across the kettle to drain; in the mean time melt a good deal of fresh butter, and bruise in either the spawn of one or two lobsters, and the meat cut small, with a spoonful of anchovy-liquor; then give it a boil, and pour it in basons. This is the best sauce: but you may make what you please. Lay the fish in the dish. Garnish with scraped horse-radish and lemon.

TO BROIL SALMON.

Cut fresh salmon in thick yieces, flour and broil them, lay them in a dish, and have plain melted butter in a cup.

TO BROIL MACKEREL WHOLE.

Cut off the heads, gut and wash them clean, pull out the roe at the neck end, boil it, then bruise it with a spoon, beat up the yolk of an egg, with a little nutmeg, a little lemon-peel cut fine, a little thyme, some parsely boiled and chopped fine, a little pepper and salt, a few crumbs of bread: mix all together, and fill the mackerel; flour it well, and broil it nicely. Let the sauce be plain butter with a little catchup or walnut pickle.

TO BROIL HERRINGS.

Scale and gut them, cut off their heads, wash them clean, dry them in a cloth, flour and broil them; take the heads and mash them, boil them in small-beer or ale, with a little whole pepper and an onion. Let it boil a quarter of an hour, strain it; thicken it with butter and flour, and a good deal of mustard. Lay the fish in a dish, and pour the sauce into a bason; or plain melted butter and mustard.

TO FRY HERRINGS.

Clean them as above, fry them in butter; have ready a good many onions peeled and cut thin; fry of a light brown with the herrings : lay the herrings in a dish, and the onions round, butter and mustard in a cup. Do them with a quick fire,

TO STEW EELS WITH BROTH.

Clean eels, put them in a saucepan with a blade or two of mace and a crust of bread. Put just water enough to cover them close, and let them stew softly; when they are enough, dish them up with the broth, and have plain melted butter and parsley in a cup to eat with them. The broth will be very good, and it is fit for weakly and consumptive constitutions.

TO DRESS A PIKE.

Gut it, and make it very clean, then turn it round with the tail in the mouth, lay it in a little dish, cut toasts three-corner ways, fill the middle with them, flour it, and stick pieces of butter all over ; then throw a little more flour, and send it to the oven : or it will do better in a tin oven before the fire, as you can baste it as you will. When it

is done lay it in a dish, and have ready melted
butter, with an anchovy dissolved in it, and a few
oysters or shrimps; and if there is any liquor in
the dish it was baked in, add to it the sauce; and
put in just what you just fancy. Pour the sauce in
the dish. Garnish it with toast about the fish, and
lemon about the dish. You should have a pudding
in the belly made thus: take grated bread, two
hard eggs chopped fine, half a nutmeg grated, a
little lemon-peel cut fine, and either the roe or liver,
or both, if any, chopped fine; and if you have
none, get either a piece of the liver of a cod, or
the roe of any fish, mix them all together with a
raw egg and a good piece of butter; roll it up and
put it into the fish's belly before you bake it. A
haddock done this way eats very well.

To broil Haddocks when they are in high Season.

Scale, gut and wash them clean; do not rip open
their bellies, but take the guts out with the gills;
dry them in a clean cloth very well: if there be
any roe or liver, take it out, but put it in again,
flour them well, and have a clear good fire. Let
the gridiron be hot and clean, lay them on, turn
them two or three times for fear of sticking; then
let one side be enough, and turn the other side,
When that is done, lay them in a dish, and have
plain butter in a cup, or anchovy and butter.

They eat finely salted a day or two before you
dress them, and hung up to dry, or boiled with egg
sauce, Newcastle is famous for salted haddocks.
They come in barrels, and keep a great while.

TO BROIL COD-SOUNDS.

You may first lay them in hot water a few

minutes; take them out, and rub them well with
salt to take off the skin and black dirt, then they
will look white; put them in water, and give them
a boil. Take them out, and flour them well, pepper
and salt them, and broil them. When they are
enough, lay them in your dish, and pour melted
butter and mustard into the dish. Broil them
whole.

TO DRESS FLAT FISH.

In dressing all sorts of flat fish, take great care
in the boiling of them; be sure to have them
enough, but do not let them be broke; mind to
put a good deal of salt in, and horse-radish in the
water; let your fish be well drained, and mind to
cut the fins off. When you fry them, let them be
well drained in a cloth, and floured, and fry them
of a fine light brown, either in oil or butter. If
there be any water in the dish with the boiled fish,
take it out with a sponge. As to fried fish, a
coarse cloth is the best thing to drain it on.

TO DRESS SALT FISH.

Old ling, which is the best sort of salt fish, lay
in water twelve hours, then lay it twelve hours on
a board, and twelve more in water. When you
boil it, put it in the water cold; if it is good, it
will take fifteen minutes boiling softly. Boil
parsnips tender, scrape them, and put them in a
saucepan; put to them some milk, stir them till
thick, then stir in a good piece of butter, and a
little salt; when they are enough, lay them in a
plate, the fish by itself dry, and butter and hard
eggs chopped in a bason.

As to water-cod, that need only be boiled and
well skimmed.

Scotch haddocks lay in water all night. You :may boil or broil them. If you broil, you must :split them in two.

You may garnish the dishes with hard eggs and]parsnips.

TO FRY LAMPREYS.

Bleed them and save the blood, then wash them iin hot water to take off the slime, and cut them to]pieces. Fry them in a little fresh butter not quite enough, pour out the fat, put in a little white wine, give the pan a shake round, season it with whole pepper, nutmeg, salt, sweet herbs, and a bay leaf; put in a few capers, a good piece of butter rolled in flour, and the blood; give the pan a shake round often, and cover them close. When they are enough, take them out, strain the sauce, then give them a boil quick, squeeze in lemon, and pour over the fish. Garnish with lemon, and dress them any way you fancy.

TO FRY EELS.

Make them very clean, cut them in pieces, season with pepper and salt, flour them, and fry them in butter. Let the sauce be plain butter melted, with the juice of lemon. Be sure they be well drained from the fat before you lay them in the dish.

TO BROIL EELS.

Take a large eel, skin and make it clean. Open the belly, cut it in four pieces; take the tail end, strip off the flesh, beat it in a mortar, season it with a little beaten mace, grated nutmeg, pepper and salt, parsley and thyme, lemon-peel, and an equal quantity of crumbs of bread; roll it in a piece of butter; then mix it again with the yolk of an egg, roll it up, and fill three pieces of belly with it. Cut the skin of the eel, wrap the pieces in, and sew up the skin. Broil them well, have butter and an anchovy for sauce, with the juice of lemon.

TO ROAST A PIECE OF FRESH STURGEON.

Get a piece of fresh sturgeon of about eight or ten pounds; let it lay in water and salt six or eight hours, with its scales on; then fasten it on the spit, and baste it well with butter for a quarter of an hour; then with a little flour, grate a nutmeg all over it, a little mace and pepper beat fine, and salt thrown over it, and a few sweet herbs dried and powdered fine, and crumbs of bread; then keep basting a little, and drudging with crumbs of bread, and with what falls from it, till it is enough. In the mean time prepare this sauce: take a pint of water, an anchovy, a little piece of lemon peel, an onion, a bundle of sweet herbs, mace, cloves, whole pepper, black and white, a piece of horse-radish; cover it close, let it boil a quarter of an hour, then strain it, put it in the saucepan again, pour in a pint of white wine, about a dozen oysters and the liquor, two spoonfuls of catchup, two of walnut pickle, the inside of a crab bruised fine, or lobster, shrimps, or prawns, a piece of butter rolled in flour, a spoonful of mushroom-pickle, or juice of lemon. Boil all together; when the fish is enough, lay it in a dish, and pour the sauce over. Garnish with fried toasts and lemons.

TO BOIL STURGEON.

Clean sturgeon, and prepare as much liquor as will just boil it. To two quarts of water, a pint of vinegar, a stick of horse-radish, two or three bits of lemon-peel, some whole pepper, and a bay leaf, add a small handful of salt. Boil the fish in this, and serve it with the following sauce: melt a pound of butter, dissolve an anchovy in it, put in a blade or two of mace, bruise the body of a crab in the butter, a few shrimps or craw-fish, a little catchup, and lemon-juice ; give it a boil, drain the fish well, and lay it in a dish. Garnish with fried oysters, sliced lemon, and scraped horse-radish; pour the sauce in boats or basons. So you may fry it, ragout it, or bake it.

TO CRIMP COD THE DUTCH WAY.

Take a gallon of pump water, a pound of salt, and mix well together ; take cod whilst alive, and cut it in slices of one inch and a half thick, throw it in the salt and water for half an hour ; then take it out and dry it well with a clean cloth, flour it and broil it ; or have a stewpan with some pump water and salt boiling, put in the fish, and boil it quick for five minutes ; send oyster, anchovy, shrimp, or what sauce you please. Garnish with horse-radish and green parsley.

TO CRIMP SCATE.

Cut it in long slips cross-ways, about an inch broad, and put it in spring water and salt as above ; then have spring water and salt boiling, put it in, and boil it fifteen minutes. Shrimp sauce, or what sauce you like.

TO BOIL SOLES.

Take three quarts of spring water, and a handful of salt; let it boil; then put in soles, boil them gently ten minutes ; then dish them up in a clean napkin, with anchovy or shrimp sauce in boats.

TO ROAST LOBSTERS.

Boil lobsters, then lay them before the fire, and baste them with butter till they have a fine froth. Dish them up with plain melted butter in a cup. This is as good a way to the full as roasting them, and not half the trouble.

TO MAKE A FINE DISH OF LOBSTERS.

Take three lobsters, boil the largest, as above, and froth it before the fire. Take the other two boiled, and butter them as in the foregoing receipt.

Take the two body shells, heat them, and fill them with the buttered meat. Lay the large one in the middle, the two shells on each side, and the two great claws of the middle lobster at each end; and the four pieces of chines of the two lobsters broiled, and laid on each end. This, if nicely done, makes a pretty dish.

TO DRESS A CRAB.

Having taken out the meat, and cleansed it from the skin, put it in a stewpan, with half a pint of white wine, a little nutmeg, pepper, and salt, over a slow fire. Throw in a few crumbs of bread, beat up the yolk of an egg with a spoonful of vinegar, throw it in, then shake the saucepan round a minute, and serve it up on a plate.

TO STEW PRAWNS, SHRIMPS, OR CRAW-FISH.

Pick out the tail, lay them by, about two quarts; take the bodies, give them a bruise, and put them in a pint of white wine, with a blade of mace; let them stew a quarter of an hour, stir them together, and strain them; then wash out the saucepan, put to it the strained liquor and tails: grate a small nutmeg in, add a little salt, and a quarter of a pound of butter rolled in flour : shake it all together ; cut a pretty thin toast round a quartern loaf, toast it brown on both sides, cut it in six pieces, lay it close together in the bottom of a dish, and pour the fish and sauce over it. Send it to table hot. If it be craw-fish or prawns, garnish the dish with some of the biggest claws laid thick round. Water will do in the room of wine, only add a spoonful of vinegar,

TO MAKE SCOLLOPS OF OYSTERS.

Put oysters into scollop-shells for that purpose, set them on a gridiron over a good clear fire, let them stew till you think they are enough, then have ready some crumbs of bread rubbed in a clean napkin, fill your shells, and set them before a good fire, and baste them well with butter. Let them be of a fine brown, keeping them turning, to be brown all over alike : but a tin oven does them best before the fire. They eat much the best done this way, though most people stew the oysters first in a saucepan, with a blade of mace, thickened with a piece of butter, and fill the shells, and then cover them with crumbs, and brown them with a hot iron : but the bread has not the fine taste of the former.

TO STEW MUSCELS.

Wash them very clean from the sand in two or three waters, put them in a stew-pan, cover them close, and let them stew till all the shells are opened ; then take them out one by one, pick them out of the shells, and look under the tongue to see if there be a crab ; if there is, you must throw away the muscel ; some only pick out the crab, and eat the muscel. When you have picked them all clean, put them in a saucepan : to a quart of muscels put half a pint of the liquor strained through a sieve, put in a blade or two of mace, a piece of butter as big as a large walnut rolled in flour ; let them stew : toast bread brown, and lay them round the dish, cut three-corner-ways ; pour in the muscels, and send them to table hot.

TO STEW SCOLLOPS.

Boil them well in salt and water, take them out and stew them in a little of the liquor, a little white wine, a little vinegar, two or three blades of mace, two or three cloves, a piece of butter rolled in flour, and the juice of a Seville orange. Stew them well, and dish them up.

MADE DISHES.

TO DRESS SCOTCH COLLOPS.

Take a piece of fillet of veal, cut it in thin pieces, as big as a crown-piece, but very thin ; shake a little flour over it, then put a little butter in a frying-pan, and melt it ; put in the collops, and fry them quick till they are brown. then lay them in a dish : have ready a good ragout made thus : take a little butter in a stewpan, and melt it, then add a large spoonful of flour, stir it about till it is smooth, then put in a pint of good brown gravy ; season it with pepper and salt, pour in a small glass of white wine, some veal sweet-breads, force-meat balls, trufflles and morels, ox palates, and mushrooms ; stew them gently for half an hour, add the juice of half a lemon to it, put it over the collops, and garnish with rashers of bacon. Some like the Scotch collops made thus : put the collops into the ragout, and stew them for five minutes.

WHITE SCOTCH COLLOPS.

Cut the veal the same as for Scotch collops, throw them in a stewpan; put boiling water over them, and stir them about, then strain them off; take a pint of good veal broth, and thicken it; add a bundle of sweet herbs, with some mace; put sweet-bread, force-meat balls, and fresh mushrooms; if no fresh to be had, use pickled ones washed in warm water; stew them fifteen minutes; add the yolk of an egg and a half, and a pint of cream: beat them well together with some nutmeg grated, and keep stirring till it boils up; add the juice of a quarter of a lemon, then put it in a dish. Garnish with lemon.

A FILLET OF VEAL WITH COLLOPS.

For an alteration, take a small fillet of veal, cut what collops you want, then take the udder and fill it with force-meat, roll it round, tie it with a pack-thread across, and roast it; lay the collops in a dish, and lay your udder in the middle. Garnish your dishes with lemon.

FORCE-MEAT BALLS.

You are to observe, that force-meat balls are a great addition to all made dishes; made thus: take half a pound of veal, and half a pound of suet, cut fine, and beat in a marble mortar or wooden bowl; have a few sweet herbs shred fine, dried mace beat fine, a small nutmeg grated, or half a large one, a little lemon peel cut very fine, a little pepper and salt, and the yolks of two eggs; mix all these well together, then roll them in little round balls, and little long balls; roll them in flour, and fry them brown. If they are for any thing of white sauce, put a little water in a saucepan, and when

the water boils put them in, and let them boil for a
few minutes, but never fry them for white sauce.

Truffles and Morels good in sauces and Soups.

Take half an ounce of truffles and morels, let
them be well washed in warm water to get the sand
and dirt out, then simmer them in two or three spoonfuls of water for a few minutes, and put them with
the liquor in the sauce. They thicken both sauce
and soup, and give it a fine flavour.

TO STEW OX PALATES.

Stew them tender; which must be done by
putting them in cold water, and let them stew softly
over a slow fire till they are tender, then take off
the two skins, cut them in pieces, and put them
either in a made-dish or soup; and cock's-combs
and artichoke-bottoms, cut small, and put in the
made-dish. Garnish the dishes with lemon, sweetbreads stewed, or white dishes, and fried for brown
ones, and cut in little pieces.

TO RAGOO A LEG OF MUTTON.

Take all the skin and fat off, cut it very thin the
right way of the grain, then butter the stewpan,
and shake flour in it: slice half a lemon and half
an onion, cut them small, with a little bundle of
sweet herbs, and a blade of mace. Put all together
with the meat in the pan, stir it a minute or two,
and then put in six spoonfuls of gravy, have ready
an anchovy minced small; mix it with butter and
flour, stir it all together for six minutes, and then
dish it up.

A BROWN FRICASEE.

You must take rabbits or chickens and skin them,

!hen cut them in small pieces, and rub them over
1with yolks of eggs. Have ready grated bread, a
llittle beaten mace and grated nutmeg, mixed toge-
!ther, and then roll them in it: put a little butter in
:a stewpan, and when it is melted put in the meat.
IFry it of a fine brown, and take care they do not
:stick to the bottom of the pan; pour the butter
lfrom them, and pour in half a pint of brown gravy,
:a glass of white wine, a few mushrooms, or two
:spoonfuls of the pickle, a little salt, if wanted, and
:a piece of butter rolled in flour. When it is of a
:fine thickness, dish it up, and send it to table.

A WHITE FRICASSEE.

Take two chickens, and cut them in small pieces,
|put them in warm water to draw out the blood,
1then in some good veal broth; if no veal broth, a
llittle boiling water, and stew them gently with a
lbundle of sweet herbs, and a blade of mace, till
:they are tender; then take out the sweet herbs, add
:a little flour and butter boiled together to thicken
:it, then add half a pint of cream, and the yolk of
:an egg beat fine; some pickled mushrooms: the
lbest way is to put fresh mushrooms in; if no fresh,
1then pickled: keep stirring it till it boils up, then
:add the juice of half a lemon, stir it well to keep it
lfrom curdling, then put it in a dish. Garnish with
llemon. Rabbits, lamb, veal, or tripe may be
(dressed the same way.

TO FRY TRIPE.

Cut tripe in long pieces of about three inches
·wide, and all the breadth of the double; put it in
·small beer-batter, or yolks of eggs: have a large

E

pan of fat, and fry it brown, then take it out, and put it to drain: dish it up with plain butter.

TO STEW TRIPE.

Cut it as you do for frying, and set on some water in a saucepan, with two or three onions cut in slices, and some salt. When it boils, put in the tripe. Ten minutes will do. Send it to table with the liquor in the dish, and the onions. Have butter and mustard in a cup, and dish it up. You may put in as many onions as you like, to mix with the sauce, or leave them quite out, just as you please.

A FRICASSEE OF PIGEONS.

Take eight pigeons, new killed, cut them in small pieces, and put them in a stewpan with a pint of claret and a pint of water. Season with salt and pepper, a blade or two of mace, an onion, a bundle of sweet herbs, a piece of butter rolled in a very little flour; cover it close, and let them stew till there is just enough for sauce, and then take out the onion and sweet herbs, beat up the yolks of three eggs, grate half a nutmeg, and with a spoon push the meat to one side of the pan, and the gravy to the other, and stir in the eggs; keep them stirring for fear of turning to curds, and when the sauce is fine and thick, shake all together, and then put the meat in the dish, pour the sauce over it, and have ready slices of bacon toasted, and fried oysters; throw the oysters all over, and lay the bacon round. Garnish with lemon.

A FRICASSEE OF LAMB-STONES AND SWEETBREADS.

Have ready lamb-stones blanched, parboiled, and sliced, and flour two or three sweetbreads; if very thick cut them in two; the yolks of six hard eggs whole; a few pastachio nut kernels, and a few large oysters; fry these all of a fine brown, then pour out all the butter, add a pint of drawn gravy, the lamb-stones, some asparagus-tops an inch long, a grated nutmeg, a little pepper and salt, two shalots shred small, and a glass of white wine. Stew all together for ten minutes, then add the yolks of three eggs beat fine, with a little white wine, and a little beaten mace; stir all together till it is of a fine thickness, and then dish it up. Garnish with lemon.

TO HASH A CALF'S HEAD.

Boil the head almost enough, then take the best half, and with a sharp knife take it nicely from the bone, with the two eyes. Lay in a little deep dish before a good fire, and take care no ashes fall into it, and then hack it with a knife cross and cross: grate nutmeg all over, the yolks of two eggs, a little pepper and salt, a few sweet herbs, crumbs of bread, and lemon-peel chopped very fine, baste it with a little butter, then baste it again; keep the dish turning, that it may be all brown alike: cut the other half and tongue in little thin bits, and set on a pint of drawn gravy in a saucepan, a little bundle of sweet herbs, an onion, pepper and salt, a glass of white wine, and two shalots; boil all these together a few minutes, strain it through a sieve, and put it in a clean stewpan with the hash. Flour the meat before you put it in, and add a few mushrooms, a spoonful of the pickle, two spoonfuls of catchup, and a few truffles and morels; stir all together for a few minutes, then beat up half

E 2

the brains, and stir in the stewpan, and a little bit
of butter rolled in flour.   Take the other half of
the brains, and beat them up with a little lemon-
peel cut fine, a little nutmeg grated, beaten mace,
thyme shred small, parsley, the yolk of an egg, and
have some good dripping boiled in a stewpan : then
fry the ·brains in little cakes, about as big as a
crown-piece,   Fry twenty oysters, dipped in the
yolk of an egg, toast some slices of bacon, fry a
few force-meat balls, and have ready a hot dish ;
if pewter, over a few coals ; if china, over a pan of
hot water.   Pour in your hash, then lay in your
toasted head, throw the force-meat balls over the
hash, and garnish the dish with fried oysters, the
fried brains, and lemon ; throw the rest over the
hash, lay the bacon round the dish, and send it to
table.

TO BAKE A CALF'S OR SHEEP'S HEAD.

Take the head, pick it, and wash it clean ; take
an earthen dish large enough to lay the head in,
rub a little piece of butter over the dish, then lay
some long iron skewers across the top of the dish,
and put the head on them ; skewer up the meat in
the middle that it do not lie on the dish, then grate
nutmeg all over it, a few sweet herbs shred small,
crumbs of· bread, a little lemon-peel cut fine, and
then flour it all over : stick pieces of butter in the
eyes, and all over the head, and flour it again.
Let it be well baked, and of a fine brown ; you
may throw pepper and salt over it, and put in the
dish a piece of beef cut small, a bundle of sweet
herbs, an onion, some whole pepper, a blade of
mace, two cloves, a pint of water, and boil the

brains with sage. When the head is enough, lay
it in a dish, and set it to the fire to keep warm, then
stir all together in the dish, and boil it in a saucepan; strain it off, put it in the saucepan again, add
a piece of butter rolled in flour, the sage in the
brains chopped fine, a spoonful of catchup, and
two spoonfuls of red wine; boil them together,
take the brains, beat them well, and mix them with
the sauce; pour it in the dish, and send it to table.
You must bake the tongue with the head, and do
not cut it out. It will lie the handsomer in the
dish.

TO DRESS A LAMB'S HEAD.

Boil the head and pluck tender, but do not let
the liver be too much done. Take the head up,
hack it cross and cross, grate some nutmeg over it,
and lay it in a dish before a good fire; then grate
some crumbs of bread, sweet herbs rubbed, a little
lemon-peel chopped fine, a very little pepper and
salt, and baste it with a little butter; then throw
flour over it, and just as it is done do the same,
baste it and drudge it. Take half the liver, the
lights, the heart, and tongue, chop them very small,
with six or eight spoonfuls of gravy or water; first
shake some flour over the meat, and stir it together,
then put in the gravy or water, a piece of butter
rolled in a little flour, a little pepper and salt, and
what runs from the head in the dish: simmer all
together a few minutes, and add half a spoonful of
vinegar, pour it in a dish, lay the head in the middle
of the mince-meat, have ready the other half of the
liver cut thin, with slices of bacon broiled, and lay
round the head. Garnish the dish with lemon, and
send it to table.

TO RAGOUT A NECK OF VEAL.

Cut a neck of veal in steaks, flatten them with a rolling pin, season with salt, pepper, cloves, and mace, lard them with bacon, lemon-peel, and thyme, dip them in the yolks of eggs; make a sheet of strong cap-paper up at the four corners, in the form of a dripping-pan; pin up the corners, butter the paper, and also the gridiron, set it over a charcoal fire: put in the meat; let it do leisurely, keep it basting and turning to keep in the gravy; and when it is enough, have ready half a pint of strong gravy, season it high, put in mushrooms and pickles, force-meat balls dipped in the yolks of eggs, oysters stewed and fried, to lay round and at the top of the dish, serve it up. If for a brown ragout, put in red wine; if white, white wine, with the yolks of eggs beat up with two or three spoonfuls of cream.

TO BOIL A LEG OF LAMB.

Let the leg be boiled very white. An hour will do it. Cut a loin in steaks, dip them in a few crumbs of bread and egg, fry them nice and brown; boil a good deal of spinage, and lay in the dish; put the leg in the middle, lay the loin round it; cut an orange in four, and garnish the dish, and have butter in a cup. Some love the spinage boiled, then drained, put in a saucepan with a piece of butter, and stewed.

TO STEW A TURKEY OR FOWL.

Let a pot be very clean, lay four skewers at the bottom, and a turkey or fowl on them, put in a quart of gravy; take a bunch of celery, cut it small and wash it clean, put it in the pot, with two or three blades of mace, let it stew softly till there is just enough for sauce, then add a piece of butter rolled in flour, two spoonfuls of red wine, two of catchup, and just as much pepper and salt as will season it; lay the fowl or turkey in the dish, pour the sauce over it, and send it to table.

If the fowl or turkey is done enough before the sauce, take it up, till the sauce is boiled enough, then put it in, let it boil a minute or two, and dish it up.

TO STEW A KNUCKLE OF VEAL.

Be sure let the pot or saucepan be clean, lay at the bottom four wooden skewers; wash and clean the knuckle very well, lay it in the pot with two or three blades of mace, a little whole pepper, a little piece of thyme, a small onion, a crust of bread, and two quarts of water. Cover close, make it boil, then only let it simmer for two hours, and when it is enough take it up, lay it in a dish, and strain the broth over it.

TO FORCE A SURLOIN OF BEEF.

When it is quite roasted, take it up, and lay it in the dish with the inside uppermost, with a sharp knife lift up the skin, hack and cut the inside very fine, shake pepper and salt over it, with two shalots, cover it with the skin, and send it to table. You may add red wine or vinegar, as you like.

BEEF A-LA-MODE.

Take a small buttock of beef, or leg-of-mutton-piece, or a piece of buttock of beef; also a dozen of cloves, eight blades of mace, and some allspice beat fine; chop a large handful of parsley, and all sorts of herbs fine; cut bacon as for beef a-la-daub, and put them in the spice and herbs, with some pepper and salt, and thrust a large pin through the beef; put it in a pot, and cover it with water; chop four large onions, and four blades of garlic very fine, six bay leaves, and a handful of champignons; put all in the pot with a pint of porter cr ale, and half a pint of red wine; cover the pot close, and stew it for six hours, according to the size of the piece; if a large piece, eight hours; then take it out, put it in a dish, cover it close, and keep it hot; take the gravy, and skim all the fat off, strain it through a sieve, pick out the champignons, and put them in the gravy; season with cayenne pepper and salt, and boil it fifteen minutes; then put the beef in a soup dish, and the gravy over it, or cut it in thin slices, and pour the liquor over it; or put it in a deep dish, with all the gravy in another: when cold, cut it in slices, and put some of the gravy round it, which will be of a strong jelly.

BEEF COLLOPS.

Take rump steaks, or any tender piece cut like Scotch collops, only larger, hack them a little with a knife, and flour them; put butter in a stewpan, and melt it, then put in the collops, and fry them quick for two minutes: put in a pint of gravy, a little butter rolled in flour, season with pepper and salt: cut four pickled cucumbers in thin slices, half a walnut, and a few capers, a little onion shred fine; stew them five minutes, then put them in a hot dish, and send them to table. You may put half a glass of white wine into it.

TO STEW BEEF STEAKS.

Take rump steaks, pepper and salt them, lay

:them in a stewpan, pour in half a pint of water, a ▸blade or two of mace, two or three cloves, a bundle ▸of sweet herbs, an anchovy, a piece of butter :rolled in flour, a glass of white wine, and an onion, ▸cover close, and let them stew softly till they are :tender; then take out the steaks, flour them, fry ▸them in fresh butter, and pour away all the fat; ▸strain the sauce they were stewed in, and pour in the pan ; toss it all up together till the sauce is hot and thick. If you add a quarter of a pint of oysters, it will make it the better. Lay the steaks in the dish, and pour the sauce over them. Garnish with any pickle you like.

TO FRY BEEF STEAKS.

Pepper and salt rump steaks, fry them in a little butter very quick and brown ; take them out, and put them into a dish, pour the fat out of the frying-pan, and then take half a pint of hot gravy; if no gravy, half a pint of hot water, and put in the pan, a little butter rolled in flour, pepper and salt, and two or three shalots chopped fine ; boil them in the pan for two minutes, then put it over the steaks and send them to table.

TO STEW A RUMP OF BEEF.

Having boiled it till it is little more than half enough, take it up, and peel of the skin : take salt pepper, beaten mace, grated nutmeg, a handful of parsley, a little thyme, winter-savory, sweet-marjoram, all chopped fine and mixed, and stuff them in great holes in the fat and lean, the rest spread over it, with the yolks of two eggs; save the gravy that runs out, put to it a pint of claret, and put the meat in a deep pan, pour the liquor in, cover close, and bake it two hours, put it in the dish, pour the liquor over it, and send it to table.

TO FRICASSEE NEATS' TONGUES BROWN.

Take neats' tongues, boil them tender, peel and cut them in thin slices, and fry them in fresh butter; then pour out the butter, put in as much gravy as you shall want for sauce, a bundle of sweet herbs, an onion, pepper and salt, and a blade or two of mace, a glass of white wine, simmer all together half an hour; take out the tongue, strain the gravy, put it with the tongue in the stewpan again, beat up the yolks of two eggs, a little grated nutmeg, a piece of butter as big as a walnut rolled in flour, shake all together for four or five minutes, dish it up, and send it to table.

TO STEW NEATS' TONGUES WHOLE.

Take two tongues, let them stew in water just to cover them for two hours, then peel them, put them in again with a pint of strong gravy, half a pint of white wine, a bundle of sweet herbs, a little pepper and salt, mace, cloves, and whole pepper, tied in a muslin rag, a spoonful of capers chopped, turnips and carrots sliced, and a piece of butter rolled in flour; let all stew together softly over a slow fire for two hours, then take out the spice and sweet herbs, and send it to table. You may leave out the turnips and carrots, or boil them by themselves, and lay them in a dish, just as you like.

To roast a Leg of Mutton with Oysters and Cockles.

Take a leg about two or three days killed, stuff it over with oysters, and roast it. Garnish with horse-radish.

A MUTTON HASH.

Cut mutton in little bits as thin as you can, strew
a little flour over it, have ready some gravy (enough
for sauce) wherein sweet herbs, onions, pepper, and
salt, have been boiled; strain it, put in the meat,
with a little piece of butter rolled in flour, and a
little salt, a shalot cut fine, a few capers and gherkins chopped fine; toss all together for a minute or
two; have ready bread toasted, and cut in thin
sippets, lay them round the dish, and pour in the
hash. Garnish the dish with pickles and horse-
radish.

Note. Some love a glass of red wine, or walnut
pickle. You may put just what you will in a hash.
If the sippets are toasted it is better,

PIG'S PETTYTOES.

Put pettytoes in a saucepan with half a pint of
water, a blade of mace, a little whole pepper, a
bundle of sweet herbs, and an onion. Let them
boil five minutes, then take out the liver, lights, and
heart, mince them very fine, grate a little nutmeg
over them, and shake flour on them; let the feet do
till they are tender, then take them out, and strain
the liquor, put all together with a little salt and a
piece of butter as big as a walnut, shake the saucepan often, let it simmer five or six minutes, then cut
toasted sippets, and lay round the dish, lay the
mince-meat and sauce in the middle, the pettytoes
split round it. You may add the juice of half a
lemon, or a little vinegar.

To dress a Leg of Mutton to eat like Venison.

Take a hind-quarter of mutton, and cut the leg
in the shape of a haunch of venison; save the

blood of the sheep, and steep it five or six hours, then take it out, and roll it in three or four sheets of white paper well buttered on the inside, tie it with packthread, and roast it, basting it with beef dripping or butter. It will take two hours at a good fire, for it must be fat and thick. Five or six minutes before you take it up, take off the paper, baste it with butter, and shake a little flour over it, to make it have a fine froth, and then have a little good drawn gravy in a bason, and sweet sauce in another. Do not garnish with any thing.

BAKED MUTTON CHOPS.

Take a loin or neck of mutton, cut it in steaks, put pepper and salt over it, butter a dish, and lay in the steaks; take a quart of milk, six eggs beat up fine, and four spoonfuls of flour; beat your flour and eggs in a little milk first, and then put the rest to it; put in a little beaten ginger, and a little salt. Pour this over the steaks, and send it to the oven; an hour and a half will bake it.

TO FRY A LOIN OF LAMB.

Cut it in chops, rub it over on both sides with the yolk of an egg, and sprinkle bread crumbs, a little parsley, thyme, marjoram, and winter-savory, chopped fine, and a little lemon-peel chopped fine; fry in butter of a nice light brown, send it in a dish by itself. Garnish with a good deal of fried parsley.

A RAGOUT OF LAMB.

Take a fore-quarter of lamb, cut the knuckle-bone off, lard it with thin bits of bacon, flour it, fry it of a fine brown, and put it in an earthen pot or stewpan: put to it a quart of broth or good gravy, a bundle of herbs, a little mace, two or three cloves, and a little whole pepper; cover close, and let it stew pretty fast for half an hour, pour the liquor all out, strain it; keep the lamb hot in the pot till the sauce is ready. Take half a pint of oysters, flour them, fry them brown, drain out all the fat clean that you fried them in, skim all the fat off the gravy; then pour it in the oysters, put in an anchovy and two spoonfuls of either red or white wine; boil all together till there is just enough for sauce, add fresh mushrooms, and some pickled ones, with a spoonful of the pickle, or the juice of half a lemon. Lay your lamb in the dish, and pour the sauce over it. Garnish with lemon.

TO STEW A LAMB'S OR CALF'S HEAD.

Wash and pick it very clean, lay it in water for an hour, take out the brains, and with a sharp pen-knife carefully take out the bones and tongue, but be careful you do not break the meat; then take out the two eyes; and take two pounds of veal and two of beef suet, a little thyme, a good piece of lemon-peel minced, a nutmeg grated, and two anchovies; chop all well together; grate two stale rolls, and mix all together with the yolks of four eggs: save enough of this meat to make about twenty balls; take half a pint of fresh mushrooms clean peeled and washed, the yolks of six eggs chopped, half a pint of oysters clean washed, or pickled cockles; mix them together; but first stew the oysters, and put to it two quarts of gravy, with a blade or two of mace. It will be proper to tie the head with packthread, cover close, and let it stew two hours: in the mean time beat up the brains with lemon-peel cut fine, a little parsley chopped, half a nutmeg grated, and the yolk of an egg; have dripping boiling, fry half the brains in little cakes, and fry the balls; keep them hot by the fire; take half an ounce of truffles and morels, then strain the gravy the head was stewed in, put the truffles and morels to it with the liquor, and a few mushrooms, boil all together, put in the rest of the brains that are not fried, stew them together for a minute or two, pour it over the head, and lay the fried brains and balls round it. Garnish with lemon. You may fry twelve oysters.

SWEETBREADS.

Do not put any water or gravy in the stewpan, but put the same veal and bacon over the sweetbreads, and season as under directed; cover close, put fire over as well as under, and when they are enough, take out the sweetbreads; put in a ladleful of gravy, boil and strain it, skim off the fat, let it boil till it jellies, then put in the sweetbreads to glaze; lay essence of ham in the dish, and the sweetbreads on it; or make a rich gravy with mushrooms, truffles and morels, a glass of white wine, and two spoonfuls of catchup. Garnish with cockscombs forced, and stewed in the gravy.

Note. You may add to the first, truffles, morels, mushrooms, cockscombs, palates, artichoke bottoms, two spoonfuls of white wine, two of catchup, or just as you please.

N.B. There are many ways of dressing sweetbreads: you may lard them with thin slips of bacon, and roast them, with what sauce you please; or you may marinate them, cut them in thin slices, flour and fry them, Serve them with fried parsley, and either butter or gravy. Garnish with lemon.

TO BOIL A HAUNCH OR NECK OF VENISON.

Lay it in salt for a week, then boil it in a cloth well floured; for every pound of venison allow a quarter of an hour for boiling. For sauce, boil cauliflowers, pulled into little sprigs, in milk and water, some fine white cabbages, turnips cut in dice, with beet-root cut in long narrow pieces, about an inch and a half long, and half an inch thick: lay a sprig of cauliflower, add some of the turnips mashed with some cream and a little butter; let cabbage be boiled, and then beat in a saucepan with a piece of butter and salt, lay that next the cauliflower, then the turnips, then cabbage, and so on, till the dish is full; place the beet-root here and there, just as you fancy; it looks very pretty, and is a fine dish. Have a little melted butter in a cup, if wanted.

Note. A leg of mutton cut venison-fashion, and dressed the same way, is a pretty dish; or a fine neck, with the scrag cut off. This eats well boiled or hashed, with gravy and sweet sauce, the next day.

TO ROAST TRIPE.

Cut tripe in two square pieces, somewhat long: have a force-meat made of crumbs of bread, pepper, salt, nutmeg, sweet herbs, lemon-peel, and the yolks of eggs, mixed together; spread it on the fat side of the tripe, and lay the other fat side next it; roll it as light as you can, and tie it with a packthread; spit it, roast it, and baste it with butter; when done, lay it on a dish; and for sauce melt butter, and add what drops from the tripe. Boil it together, and garnish with raspings.

TO DRESS POULTRY.

TO ROAST A TURKEY.

The best way to roast a turkey, is to loosen the skin on the breast, and fill it with force-meat, made thus: take a quarter of a pound of beef suet, as many crumbs of bread, a little lemon-peel, and anchovy, some nutmeg, pepper, parsley, and thyme. Chop and beat them all well together, mix them with the yolk of an egg, and stuff up the breast; when you have no suet, butter will do : or make force-meat thus : spread bread and butter thin, and grate nutmeg over it ; when you have enough, roll it up, and stuff the breast of the turkey ; then roast it of a fine brown, but be sure to pin white paper on the breast till it is near done enough.   You must have good gravy in the dish, and bread sauce made thus: take a good piece of crumb, put it in a pint of water, with a blade or two of mace, two or three cloves, and some whole pepper. Boil it up five or six times, then with a spoon take out the spice you had before put in, and pour off the water; (you may boil an onion in it if you please ;) then beat up the bread with a good piece of butter and a little salt.   Or onion sauce made thus : take onions, peel them, and cut them in thin slices, and boil them half an hour in milk and water; then drain the water from them, and beat them up with a good piece of butter; shake a little flour in, and stir it all together with a little cream, if you have it (or milk will do ;) put the sauce into boats, and garnish with lemon.

Another way to make sauce : take half a pint of oysters, strain the liquor, and put the oysters with the liquor in a saucepan, with a blade or two of mace, let them just lump, pour in a glass of white wine, let it boil once, and thicken it with a piece of butter rolled in flour. Serve this up by itself, with good gravy in the dish, for every body does not love oyster-sauce. This makes a pretty side dish for supper, or a corner dish of a table for dinner. If you chafe it in a dish, add half a pint of gravy to it, and boil it up together.

To make Mushroom Sauce for White Fowls of all sorts.

Take a quart of fresh mushrooms, well cleaned and washed, cut them in two, put them in a stew-pan, with a little butter, a blade of mace, and a little salt; stew it gently for an hour, then add a pint of cream, and the yolks of two eggs beat very well, and keep stirring till it boils up; then squeeze half a lemon, put it over the fowls, or turkeys, or in basons or in a dish, with a piece of French bread first buttered, then toasted brown, and just dip it in boiling water; put it in the dish, and the mushrooms over.

Mushroom Sauce for White Fowls boiled.

Take half a pint of cream, and a quarter of a pound of butter, stir them together one way till it is thick; then add a spoonful of mushroom pickle, pickled mushrooms, or fresh, if you have them. Garnish only with lemon.

To make Celery Sauce, either for roasted or boiled Fowls, Turkeys, Partridges, or any other Game.

Take a large bunch of celery, wash and pare it clean, cut it in little thin bits, and boil it softly in a little water till it is tender; then add a little beaten

mace, nutmeg, pepper and salt, thickened with a
piece of butter rolled in flour; then boil it up, and
pour it in a dish.

You may make it with cream thus: boil celery
as above, and add mace, nutmeg, a piece of butter
as big as a walnut rolled in flour, and half a pint
of cream; boil all together.

To make Egg Sauce proper for roasted Chickens.

Melt butter thick and fine, chop two or three
hard boiled eggs fine, put them in a bason, pour
the butter over them, and have good gravy in
the dish.

TO STEW A TURKEY BROWN.

Take a turkey after it is nicely picked and drawn,
fill the skin of the breast with force-meat, and put
an anchovy, a shalot, and thyme in the belly; lard
the breast with bacon; then put a piece of butter
in the stewpan, flour the turkey, and fry it just of
a fine brown; then take it out, and put it in a deep
stewpan, or a little pot that will just hold it, and
put in as much gravy as will barely cover it, a glass
of white wine, some whole pepper, mace, two or
three cloves, and a little bundle of sweet herbs;
cover close, and stew it for an hour; then take up
the turkey, and keep it hot, covered, by the fire;
and boil the sauce to about a pint, strain it off, add
the yolks of two eggs, and a piece of butter rolled
in flour; stir it till it is thick, and then lay the turkey
in the dish, and pour the sauce over it. You may
have ready some little French loaves, about the
bigness of an egg, cut off the tops, and take out
the crumbs, then fry them of a fine brown, fill them
with stewed oysters, lay them round the dish, and
garnish with lemon.

TO FORCE A FOWL.

Take a good fowl, pick and draw it, slit the skin down the back, and take the flesh from the bones, mince it very small, and mix it with one pound of beef-suet shred fine, a pint of large oysters chopped, two anchovies, a shalot, a little grated bread, and sweet herbs; shred all this well, mix them together, and make it up with the yolks of eggs; turn all these ingredients on the bones again, draw the skin over, and sew up the back, and either boil the fowl in a bladder an hour and a quarter, or roast it; then stew more oysters in gravy, bruise in a little of the force-meat, mix it up with a little fresh butter, and a very little flour; then give it a boil, lay the fowl in a dish, and pour the sauce over it. Garnish with lemon.

TO BROIL CHICKENS.

Slit them down the back, and season with pepper and salt, lay them on a very clear fire, and at a great distance. Let the inside lie next the fire till it is above half done; then turn it, and take great care the fleshy side does not burn, and let them be of a fine brown. Let the sauce be good gravy, with mushrooms, and garnish with lemon and the livers broiled, the gizzards cut, slashed, and broiled with pepper and salt.

Or this sauce: take a handful of sorrel, dipped in boiling water, drain it, and have ready half a pint of good gravy, a shalot shred small, and parsley boiled green: thicken it with a piece of butter rolled in flour, and add a glass of red wine, lay the sorrel in heaps round the fowls, and pour the sauce over them. Garnish with lemon.

Note. You may make just what sauce you fancy.

F

Chickens with Tongues. A good Dish for a great deal of Company

Take six small chickens boiled very white, six hogs' tongues, boiled and peeled, a cauliflower boiled in milk and water whole, and a good deal of spinage boiled green; then lay the cauliflower in the middle, the chickens close all round, and the tongues round them with the roots outward, and the spinage in little heaps between the tongues. Garnish with little pieces of bacon toasted, and lay a piece on each of the tongues.

TO BOIL A DUCK OR A RABBIT WITH ONIONS.

Boil a duck or rabbit in a good deal of water; be sure to skim the water, for there will always rise a scum, which, if it boils down, will discolour fowls, &c. They will take about half an hour boiling. For sauce, onions must be peeled, and thrown in water as you peel them, then cut them in thin slices, boil them in milk and water, and skim the liquor. Half an hour will boil them. Throw them in a clean sieve to drain, put them in a saucepan, and chop them small, shake in a little flour, put in two or three spoonfuls of cream, a good piece of butter, stew all together over the fire till they are thick and fine, lay the duck or rabbit in the dish, and pour the sauce all over : if a rabbit, cut off the head; cut it in two, and lay it on each side the dish.

Or you make this sauce for change : take a large onion, cut it small, half a handful of parsley clean washed and picked, chop it small, a lettuce cut small, a quarter of a pint of good gravy, a piece of butter rolled in a little flour; add a little juice of lemon, a little pepper and salt; stew all together for half an hour, then add two spoonfuls of red wine. This sauce is most proper for a duck; lay the duck in the dish, and pour the sauce over it.

A DUCK WITH GREEN PEAS.

Put a deep stewpan over the fire, with a piece of fresh butter; singe the duck, and flour it, turn it in the pan two or three minutes, pour out all the fat, but let the duck remain in the pan: put to it a pint of good gravy, a pint of peas, two lettuces cut small, a bundle of sweet herbs, a little pepper and salt, cover close, and let them stew for half an hour; now and then give the pan a shake; when they are just done, grate in a little nutmeg, and put in a little beaten mace, and thicken it, either with a piece of butter rolled in flour, or the yolk of an egg beat up with two or three spoonfuls of cream; shake it all together for three or four minutes, take out the sweet herbs, lay the duck in a dish, and pour the sauce over it. You may garnish with boiled mint chopped, or let it alone.

Directions for roasting a Goose.

Take sage, wash and pick it clean, and an onion, chop them fine, with pepper and salt, and put them in the belly; let the goose be clean picked, and wiped dry with a cloth, inside and out; put it down to the fire, and roast it brown: one hour will roast a large goose, three quarters of an hour a small one. Serve it in a dish with brown gravy, apple sauce in a boat, and some gravy in another.

TO STEW GIBLETS.

Let them be nicely scalded and picked, cut the pinions in two; cut the head, neck, and legs in two and the gizzards in four; wash them very clean; put them in a stewpan or soup-pot, with three pounds of scrag of veal; just cover them with water; let them boil up, take all the scum clean off; then put three onions, two turnips, one carrot, a little thyme and parsley, stew them till they are tender, strain them through a sieve, wash the giblets clean with warm water out of the herbs, &c.; then take a piece of butter as big as a large walnut, put it in a stewpan, melt it, and put in a large spoonful of flour, keep it stirring till it is smooth; then put in the broth and giblets, stew them for a quarter of an hour; season with salt: or you may add a gill of Lisbon; and just before you serve them up, chop a handful of green parsley, and put in; give them a boil up, and serve them in a tureen or soup dish.

N. B. Three pair will make a handsome tureen full.

TO BOIL PIGEONS.

Boil them by themselves for fifteen minutes; boil a handsome square piece of bacon, and lay it in the middle: stew spinage to lay round, and lay the pigeons on the spinage. Garnish with parsley laid in a plate before the fire to crisp. Or lay one pigeon in the middle, and the rest round, and the spinage between each pigeon, and a slice of bacon on each pigeon. Garnish with slices of bacon, and melted butter in a cup.

TO JUG PIGEONS.

Pull, crop, and draw pigeons, but do not wash them; save the livers, and put them in scalding water, set them on the fire for a minute or two;

then take them out, and mince them small, bruise them with the back of a spoon; mix them with a little pepper, salt, grated nutmeg, and lemon-peel shred very fine, chopped parsley, and two yolks of hard eggs; bruise them as you do the liver, and put as much suet as liver, shaved fine, and as much grated bread; work them together with raw eggs, and roll it in fresh butter; put a piece in the crops and bellies, and sew up the necks and vents; then dip the pigeons in water, and season with pepper and salt, as for a pie, put them in the jug with a piece of celery, stop them close, and set them in a kettle of cold water; first cover them close, and lay a tile on the top of the jug, and let it boil three hours; then take them out of the jug, and lay them in a dish, take out the celery, put in a piece of butter rolled in flour, shake it till it is thick, and pour it on the pigeons. Garnish with lemon.

TO STEW PIGEONS.

Season pigeons with pepper and salt, a few cloves and mace, and sweet herbs; wrap this seasoning up in a piece of butter, and put it in their bellies; then tie up the neck and vent, and half roast them; put them in a stewpan, with a quart of good gravy, a little white wine, a few pepper corns, three or four blades of mace, a bit of lemon, a bundle of sweet herbs, and a small onion; stew them gently till they are enough; then take the pigeons out, and strain the liquor through a sieve; skim it, and thicken it in the pan, put in the pigeons, with pickled mushrooms and oysters; stew it five minutes, and put the dish, and the sauce over.

F 3

TO ROAST PARTRIDGES.

Let them be nicely roasted, but not too much ;
baste them gently with a little butter, and drudge
with flour, sprinkle a little salt on, and froth them
nicely up ; have good gravy in a dish, with bread-
sauce in a boat, made thus : take a handful or two
of crumbs of bread, put in a pint of milk, or more,
a small whole onion, a little whole white pepper, a
little salt, and a bit of butter ; boil it all up ; then
take the onion out, and beat it well with a spoon ;
take poverroy sauce in a boat, made thus : chop
four shalots fine, a gill of good gravy, a spoonful
of vinegar, a little pepper and salt ; boil them up
one minute, then put it in a boat.

TO ROAST PHEASANTS.

Pick and draw pheasants, singe them ; lard one
with bacon, but not the other; spit them, roast them
fine, and paper them all over the breast : when they
are just done, flour and baste them with a little
nice butter, and let them have a fine white froth :
then take them up, and pour good gravy in the
dish, and bread-sauce in plates.

TO BOIL A PHEASANT.

Take a fine pheasant, boil it in a good deal of
water, keep the water boiling; half an hour will
do a small one, and three quarters of an hour a
large one. Let the sauce be celery stewed and
thickened with cream, and a little piece of butter
rolled in flour ; take up the pheasant, and pour the
sauce over. Garnish with lemon. Observe to
stew celery so, that the liquor will not be all wasted
away before you put the cream in ; if it wants salt,
put in some to your palate.

TO ROAST SNIPES OR WOODCOCKS.

Spit them on a small bird-spit, flour and baste them with a piece of butter, have ready a slice of bread, toasted brown, lay it in a dish, and set it under the snipes for the trail to drop on ; when they are enough, take them up, and lay them on a toast ; have ready for two snipes a quarter of a pint of good gravy and butter ; pour it in the dish, and set it over a chafing-dish two or three minutes. Garnish with lemon, and send to table.

TO DRESS PLOVERS.

To two plovers take two artichoke bottoms boiled, chesnuts roasted and blanched, some skirrets boiled, cut all very small, mix it with some marrow or beef-suet, the yolks of two hard eggs, chop all together ; season with pepper, salt, nutmeg, and a little sweet herbs ; fill the bodies of the plovers, lay them in a saucepan, put to them a pint of gravy, a glass of white wine, a blade or two of mace, some roasted chesnuts blanched, and artichoke bottoms cut in quarters, two or three yolks of eggs, and a little juice of lemon ; cover close, and let them stew an hour softly. If you find the sauce is not thick enough, take a piece of butter rolled in flour, and put into the sauce ; shake it round, and when it is thick, take up your plovers, and pour the sauce over them. Garnish with roasted chesnuts.

Ducks are very good done this way.

Or you may roast plovers as you do any other fowl, and have gravy sauce in the dish.

Or boil them in good celery sauce, either white or brown, as you like.

The same way you may dress widgeons.

N.B. The best way to dress plovers, is to roast them as woodcocks, with a toast under them, and gravy and butter.

TO DRESS A JUGGED HARE.

Cut it in little pieces, lard them here and there with little slips of bacon, season with a little pepper and salt, put them in an earthen jug, with a blade or two of mace, an onion stuck with cloves, and a bundle of sweet herbs; cover the jug close that nothing can get in, then set it in a pot of boiling water, and three hours will do it; then turn it out in the dish, and take out the onion and sweet herbs, and send it to table hot. If you do not like it larded, leave it out.

TO BOIL RABBITS.

Truss them for boiling, boil them quick and white; put them in a dish, with onion sauce over, made thus: take as many onions as you think will cover them; peel them, and boil them tender, strain them off, squeeze them very dry, and chop them fine; put them in a stewpan, with a piece of butter, half a pint of cream, a little salt, and shake in a little flour; stir them well over a gentle fire, till the butter is melted; then put them over the rabbits: or a sauce made thus: blanch the livers, and chop them very fine, with some parsley blanched and chopped; mix them with melted butter, and put it over; or with gravy and butter.

COD SOUNDS BROILED WITH GRAVY.

Scald them in hot water, and rub them with salt well; blanch them; that is, take off the black dirty skin, set them on in cold water, and let them simmer till they begin to be tender; take them out aud flour them, and broil them on the gridiron. In the mean time take good gravy, mustard, a bit of butter rolled in flour, boil it, season it with pepper and salt. Lay the sounds in a dish, and pour the sauce over them.

FRIED SAUSAGES.

Take half a pound of sausages, and six apples, slice four as thick as a crown, cut the other two in quarters, fry them with the sausages of a fine light brown, lay the sausages in the middle of the dish, and the apples round. Garnish with the quartered apples.

Stewed cabbage and sausages fried is a good dish ; then heat cold peas-pudding in the pan, lay it in a dish, and the sausages round, heap the pudding in the middle, and lay the sausages round thick up, edge-ways, and one in the middle at length.

COLLOPS AND EGGS.

Cut either bacon, pickled beef, or hung mutton, in thin slices, broil them nicely, lay them in a dish before the fire, have ready a stewpan of water boiling, break as many eggs as you have collops, one by one in a cup, and pour them in a stewpan. When the whites of the eggs begin to harden, and all look of a clear white, take them up one by one in an egg-slice, and lay them on the collops.

TO DRESS COLD FOWL OR PIGEON.

Cut them in four quarters, beat up an egg or two, according to what you dress, grate in nutmeg, a little salt, parsley chopped, a few crumbs of bread; beat them well together, dip them in this batter, and have ready dripping, hot in a stewpan, in which fry them of a fine light brown; have ready a little good gravy, thickened with a little flour, mixed with a spoonful of catchup: lay the fry in the dish, and pour the sauce over. Garnish with lemon, and a few mushrooms, if you have any. A cold rabbit eats well done thus.

TO MINCE VEAL.

Cut veal as fine as possible, but do not chop it; grate nutmeg over it, shred a little lemon-peel very fine, throw a very little salt on it, drudge a little flour over it. To a large plate of veal take four or five spoonsful of water, let it boil, then put in the veal, with a bit of butter as big as an egg, stir it well together; when it is quite hot, it is enough. Have ready a thin piece of bread, toasted brown, cut it in three corner sippets, lay it round the plate, and pour in the veal. Before you pour it in, squeeze in half a lemon, or half a spoonful of vinegar. Garnish with lemon. You may put gravy instead of water, if you love it strong; but it is better without.

TO FRY COLD VEAL.

Cut it in pieces about as thick as half-a-crown, and as long as you please, dip them in the yolk of eggs, and then in crumbs of bread, with sweet herbs and shred lemon-peel in it; grate a little nutmeg over them, and fry them in fresh butter. The butter must be hot, just enough to fry them in: in the mean time, make gravy of the bone of the veal. When the meat is fried, take it out with a fork, and lay it in a dish before the fire; then shake flour in the pan, and stir it round; then put in a little gravy, squeeze in a little lemon, and pour it over the veal. Garnish with lemon.

TO TOSS UP COLD VEAL WHITE.

Cut the veal in little thin bits, put milk enough to it for sauce, grate in a little nutmeg, a little salt, a little piece of butter rolled in flour: to half a pint of milk, the yolks of two eggs well beat, a spoonful of mushroom pickle; stir all together till it is thick, then pour it in a dish, and garnish with lemon.

Cold fowls skimmed, and done this way, eat well; or the best end of a cold breast of veal; first fry it, drain it from this fat, then pour the sauce to it.

TO HASH COLD MUTTON.

Cut mutton with a very sharp knife in little bits, as thin as possible; then boil the bones with an onion, a few sweet herbs, a blade of mace, a very little whole pepper, a little salt, a piece of crust toasted crisp; let it boil till there is enough for sauce, strain it, and put it in a saucepan with a piece of butter rolled in flour; put in the meat; when it is very hot it is enough. Have ready thin bread, toasted brown, cut three-corner-ways, lay them round the dish, and pour in the hash. As to walnut pickle, and all sorts of pickles, you must put in according to your fancy. Garnish with pickles. Some love a small onion peeled, and cut very small, and done in the hash.

TO HASH MUTTON LIKE VENISON.

Cut it thin as above; boil the bones as above; strain the liquor, where there is just enough for the hash; to a quarter of a pint of gravy put a large spoonful of red wine, an onion peeled and chopped fine, a little lemon-peel shred fine, a piece of butter as big as a small walnut, rolled in flour: put it in a saucepan with the meat, shake it together, and when it is thoroughly hot, pour it in a dish. Hash beef the same way.

TO MAKE COLLOPS OF COLD BEEF.

If you have any cold inside of a surloin of beef, take off all the fat, cut it in little thin bits, cut an onion small, boil as much water or gravy as you think will do for sauce; season it with a little pepper and salt, and sweet herbs. Let the water boil, then put in the meat, with a piece of butter rolled in flour, shake it round, and stir it. When the sauce is thick, and the meat done, take out the sweet herbs, and pour it in a dish. They do better than fresh meat.

Rules to be observed in all Made Dishes.

First, let the stewpans, or saucepans, and covers, be very clean, free from sand, and well tinned; and that all the white sauces have a little tartness, and be very smooth, and of a fine thickness; and all the time any white sauce is over the fire, keep stirring it one way.

And as to brown sauce, take care no fat swims at the top, but that it be all smooth alike, and about as thick as good cream, and not to taste of one thing more than another. As to pepper and salt, season to your palate, but do not put too much, for that will take away the fine flavour of every thing. As to most made-dishes, put in what you think proper to enlarge it, or make it good; as mushrooms pickled, dried, fresh, or powdered; truffles, morels, cockscombs stewed, ox-palates cut in small bits; artichoke bottoms, either pickled, fresh, boiled, or dried, softened in warm water, each cut in four pieces; asparagus tops, the yolks of hard eggs, force-meat balls, &c. The best things to give a sauce tartness are mushroom pickle, white walnut pickle, elder vinegar, or lemon juice.

OF SOUPS AND BROTHS.

STRONG BROTH FOR SOUP AND GRAVY.

Take a shin of beef, a knuckle of veal, and a scrag of mutton, put them in five gallons of water; let it boil up, skim it clean, and season with six large onions, four leeks, four heads of celery, two carrots, two turnips, a bundle of sweet herbs, six cloves, a dozen corns of allspice, and salt; skim it very clean, and let it stew gently for six hours; strain it off, and put it by for use.

When you want very strong gravy, take a slice of bacon, lay it in a stewpan; a pound of beef, cut it thin, lay it on the bacon, slice in a piece of carrot, an onion sliced, a crust of bread, a few sweet herbs, a little mace, cloves, nutmeg, whole pepper, and an anchovy; cover and set it on a slow fire five or six minutes, and pour in a quart of the above gravy: cover close, and let it boil softly till half is wasted. This will be a rich, high, brown sauce for fish, fowl, or ragout.

GRAVY FOR WHITE SAUCE.

Take a pound of any part of veal, cut it in small pieces, boil it in a quart of water, with an onion, a blade of mace, two cloves, and a few whole pepper-corns. Boil it till it is as rich as you would have it.

GRAVY FOR TURKEY, FOWL, OR RAGOUT.

Take a pound of lean beef, cut and hack it well, then flour it, put a piece of butter as big as a hen's egg in a stewpan; when it is melted, put in the beef, fry it on all sides a little brown, then pour in three pints of boiling water, a bundle of sweet herbs, two or three blades of mace, three or four cloves, twelve whole pepper-corns, a bit of carrot, a piece of crust of bread toasted brown; cover close, and let it boil till there is about a pint or less; season it with salt, and strain it off.

MUTTON OR VEAL GRAVY.

Cut and hack veal well, set it on the fire with water, sweet herbs, mace, and pepper. Let it boil till it is as good as you would have it, then strain it off. Your fine cooks, if they can, chop a partridge or two, and put in gravies.

A STRONG FISH GRAVY.

Take two or three eels, or any fish you have, skin or scale them, gut and wash them from grit, cut them in little pieces, put them in a saucepan, cover them with water, a little crust of bread toasted brown, a blade or two of mace, and some whole pepper, a few sweet herbs, and a little bit of lemon-peel. Let it boil till it is rich and good, then have ready a piece of butter, according to the gravy; if a pint, as big as a walnut. Melt it in the saucepan, shake in a little flour, and toss it about till it is brown, and strain in the gravy. Let it boil a few minutes, and it will be good.

STRONG BROTH TO KEEP FOR USE.

Take part of a leg of beef, and the scrag end of a neck of mutton, break the bones in pieces, and put to it as much water as will cover it, and a little salt; skim it clean, and put in a whole onion stuck with cloves, a bunch of sweet herbs, pepper, and a nutmeg quartered. Boil these till the meat is in pieces and the strength boiled out; strain it and keep it for use.

GREEN PEAS SOUP.

Take a gallon of water, make it boil; put in six onions, four turnips, two carrots, two heads of celery, cut in slices, some cloves, four blades of mace, four cabbage-lettuces cut small; stew them for an hour; strain it off, and put in two quarts of old green peas, and boil them in the liquor till tender; then beat or bruise them, and mix them up with the broth, and rub them through a tammy or cloth, and put it in a clean pot, and boil it up fifteen minutes; season with pepper and salt to your liking; then put the soup in a tureen, with small dices of bread toasted very hard.

A PEAS SOUP FOR WINTER.

Take about four pounds of lean beef, cut it in small pieces, a pound of lean bacon, or pickled pork, set it on the fire with two gallons of water, let it boil, and skim it well; then put in six onions, two turnips, one carrot, and four heads of celery, cut small, twelve corns of allspice, and put in a quart of split peas, boil it gently for three hours, strain them through a sieve, and rub the peas well through; then put the soup in a clean pot, and put in dried mint rubbed to powder; cut the white of four heads of celery, and two turnips in dices, and boil them in a quart of water for fifteen minutes; strain them off, and put them in the soup; take a dozen of small rashers of bacon fried, and put them in the soup, season with pepper and salt to your liking;

boil it up for fifteen minntes, then put it in a tureen, with dices of bread fried crisp.

Note.   The liquor of a boiled leg of pork makes good soup.

MUTTON BROTH.

Take a neck of mutton of six pounds, cut it in two, boil the scrag in a gallon of water, skim it well, put in a little bundle of sweet herbs, an onion, and a good crust of bread.   Let it boil an hour, then put in the other part of the mutton, a turnip or two, dried marigolds, a few chives chopped fine, a little parsley chopped small; put these in a quarter of an hour before the broth is enough. Season it with salt; or you may put in a quarter of a pound of barley or rice at first.   Some love it thickened with oatmeal, and some with bread; others, season with mace, instead of sweet herbs and onion.   All this is fancy, and different palates. If you boil turnips for sauce, do not boil all in the pot, it makes the broth too strong of them, but boil them in a saucepan.

BEEF BROTH.

Take a leg of beef, crack the bone in two or three parts, wash it clean, put it in a pot with a gallon of water, skim it, put in two or three blades of mace, a bundle of parsley, and a crust of bread. Boil it till the beef is tender, and the sinews. Toast bread, and cut it in dices, put it in a tureen; lay in the meat, and pour in the soup.

SCOTCH BARLEY BROTH.

Take a leg of beef, chop it to pieces, boil it in three gallons of water, with a piece of carrot and a crust of bread, till it is half boiled away; strain it off, and put it in the pot again with half a pound of barley, four or five heads of celery, washed clean, and cut small, a large onion, a bundle of sweet herbs, a little parsley chopped small, and a few marygolds. Boil this an hour. Take a cock, or large fowl, clean picked and washed, put it in the pot; boil it till the broth is good, season it with salt, and send it to table with the fowl in the middle. This broth is very good without the fowl. Take out the onion and sweet herbs before you send it to table.

Some make this broth with sheep's head instead of a leg of beef, and it is very good: but you must chop the head to pieces. The thick flank (six pounds to six quarts of water) makes good broth: then put the barley in with the meat, first skim it well, boil it an hour very softly, then put in the above ingredients, with turnips and carrots clean scraped and pared, and cut in pieces. Boil all together softly, till the broth is good; season it with salt, and send it to table, with the beef in the middle, turnips and carrots round, and pour the broth over all.

Rules to be observed in making Soups or Broths.

Take great care the pots, saucepans, and covers, be very clean, and free from grease and sand, and that they be well tinned, for fear of giving the broths and soups any brassy taste. If you have time to stew as softly as you can, it will both have a finer flavor, and the meat will be tenderer. But then observe, when you make soups or broths for present use, if it is to be done softly, do not put more water than you intend to have soup or broth;

and if you have the convenience of an earthen
pan, or pipkin, set it on wood embers till it boils,
then skim it, and put in the seasoning; cover close,
and set it on embers, so that it may do softly for
some time, and the meat and broths will be delicious. Observe, in all broths and soups, that one
thing does not taste more than another, but that
the taste be equal, and it has a fine agreeable re-
lish, according to what you design it for; and be
sure that all the greens and herbs you put in be
cleaned, washed, and picked.

OF PUDDINGS.

A MARROW PUDDING.

Take a quart of cream and milk, and a quarter
of a pound of Naples biscuit, put them on the fire
in a stewpan, and boil them up; take the yolk of
eight eggs, the whites of four, beat very fine, a little
soft sugar, some marrow chopped, a small glass of
brandy and sack, a little orange-flower-water; mix
all well together, and put them on the fire, keep
stirring till it is thick, and put it away to get cold;
have a dish rimmed with puff-paste, put your stuff
in, sprinkle currants that have been well washed in
cold water, and rubbed clean in a cloth, marrow
cut in slices, and some candied lemon, orange and
citron, cut in shreds, and send it to the oven; three
quarters of an hour will bake it : send it up hot.

A BOILED SUET PUDDING.

A quart of milk, four spoonfuls of flour, a pound
of suet, shred small, four eggs, a spoonful of beaten
ginger, a tea-spoonful of salt: mix the eggs and
flour with a pint of the milk very thick, and with

the seasoning mix in the rest of the milk and suet.
Let the batter be thick, and boil it two hours.

A BOILED PLUMB PUDDING.

Take a pound of suet cut in pieces, not too fine,
a pound of currants, and a pound of raisins stoned,
eight eggs, half the whites, half a nutmeg grated,
and a tea-spoonful of beaten ginger, a pound of
flour, a pint of milk; beat the eggs first, add half
the milk, beat them together, and by degrees stir
in the flour, then the suet, spice, and fruit, and as
much milk as will mix it together very thick. Boil
it five hours.

A YORKSHIRE PUDDING.

Take a quart of milk, four eggs, and a little salt,
make it up in a thick batter with flour, like pancake
batter. Have a good piece of meat at the fire:
take a stewpan, and put some dripping in, set it on
the fire; when it boils, pour in the pudding; let it
bake on the fire till you think it is nigh enough,
then turn a plate upside down in the dripping-pan,
that the dripping may not be blacked; set the stewpan on it, under the meat, and let the dripping
drop on the pudding, and the heat of the fire come
to it, to make it of a fine brown. When the meat
is done and sent to table, drain the fat from the
pudding, and set it on the fire to dry a little; then
slide it as dry as you can in a dish; melt butter,
and pour it in a cup, and set it in the middle of the
pudding. It is an excellent good pudding; the
gravy of the meat eats well with it.

A STEAK PUDDING.

Make a good crust, with suet shred fine with
flour, and mix it with cold water: season with a

G

little salt, and make a pretty stiff crust, about two pounds of suet to a quarter of a peck of flour. Let the steaks be either beef or mutton, well seasoned with pepper and salt; make it up as you do an apple pudding; tie it in a cloth, and put it in the water boiling. If it be large, it will take five hours; if small three hours. This is the best crust for an apple pudding. Pigeons eat well this way.

SUET DUMPLINGS.

Take a pint of milk, four eggs, a pound of suet, a pound of currants, two tea-spoonfuls of salt, three of ginger: first take half the milk, and mix it like a thick batter, then put the eggs, the salt, and ginger, then the rest of the milk by degrees, with the suet and currants, and flour, to make it like a light paste. When the water boils, make them in rolls as big as a large turkey's egg, with a little flour; then flat them and throw them in boiling water. Move them softly, that they do not stick together; keep the water boiling, and half an hour will boil them.

A POTATOE PUDDING.

Boil two pounds of potatoes, and beat them in a mortar fine, beat in half a pound of melted butter, boil it half an hour, pour melted butter over it, with a glass of white wine, or the juice of a Seville orange, and throw sugar over it and the dish.

TO BOIL AN ALMOND PUDDING.

Beat a pound of sweet-almonds as small as possible, with three spoonfuls of rose-water, and a gill of sack or white wine, and mix in half a pound of fresh butter melted, five yolks of eggs and two whites, a quart of cream, a quarter of a pound of sugar, half a nutmeg grated, one spoonful of flour, and three of crumbs of bread; mix all well together, and boil it. It will take half an hour boiling.

A SAGO PUDDING.

Let half a pound of sago be washed in three or four hot waters, put to it a quart of new milk, and let it boil together till it is thick; stir it carefully, (for it is apt to burn,) put in a stick of cinnamon when you set it on the fire; when it is boiled take it out; before you pour it out, stir in half a pound of fresh butter, then pour it in a pan, and beat up nine eggs, with five of the whites and four spoonfuls of sack; stir all together, and sweeten to your taste. Put in a quarter of a pound of currants, washed and rubbed, and plumped in two spoonfuls of sack, and two of rose-water; mix all together, stir it over a slow fire till it is thick, lay a puff paste over a dish, pour in the ingredients, and bake it.

A MILLET PUDDING.

You must get half a pound of millet-seed, after it is washed and picked clean, put to it half a pound of sugar, a whole nutmeg grated, and three quarts of milk. When you have mixed all well together, break in half a pound of fresh butter in your dish, pour it in, and bake it.

AN APPLE PUDDING.

Take twelve large pippins, pare them, take out the cores, and put them in a saucepan, with four or five spoonfuls of water; boil them till they are soft and thick; beat them well, stir in a pound of loaf sugar, the juice of three lemons, the peel of two lemons cut thin, and beat fine in a mortar, the yolks of eight eggs beat: mix all together, bake it.

in a slack oven ; when it is near done, throw over
a little fine sugar. You may bake it in a puff-paste,
as you do the other puddings.

A RICE PUDDING.

. In half a pound of rice put three quarts of milk,
stir in half a pound of sugar, grate in a small nutmeg, and break in half a pound of fresh butter ;
butter a dish, pour it in, and bake it. You may add
a quarter of a pound of currants for change. If you
boil the rice and milk, and then stir in the sugar, you
may bake it before the fire, or in a tin oven. You
may add eggs, but it will be good without.

TO BOIL A CUSTARD PUDDING.

Take a pint of cream, out of which take two or
three spoonfuls, and mix with a spoonful of fine
flour ; set the rest to boil. When it is boiled, take
it off, and stir in the cold cream and flour well ;
when cold, beat up five yolks and two whites of
eggs, and stir in a little salt and nutmeg, and two
or three spoonfuls of sack ; sweeten to your
palate ; butter a wooden bowl, and pour it in, tie
a cloth over it, and boil it half an hour. When it
is enough, untie the cloth, turn the pudding in a
dish, and pour melted butter over it.

A BATTER PUDDING.

Take a quart of milk, beat up six eggs, half the
whites, mix as above, six spoonfuls of flour, a tea-
spoonful of salt, and one of beaten ginger : mix all
together, boil it an hour and a quarter, and pour
melted butter over it. You may put in eight eggs,
for change, and half a pound of prunes or currants.

A BATTER PUDDING WITHOUT EGGS.

Take a quart of milk, mix six spoonfuls of flour
with a little of the milk first, a tea-spoonful of salt,

two of beaten ginger, and two of the tincture of saffron; mix all together, and boil it an hour. You may add fruit as you think proper.

A BREAD PUDDING.

Cut off all the crust of a twopenny loaf, and slice it thin in a quart of milk, set it over a chafing-dish of coals till the bread has soaked up the milk, then put in a piece of sweet butter, stir it round, let it stand till cold; or you may boil the milk, and pour over the bread, and cover close, it does full as well; then take the yolks of six eggs, the whites of three, and beat them up with a little rose-water and nutmeg, if you choose it. Mix all well together, and boil it one hour.

A BAKED BREAD PUDDING.

Take the crumb of a two-penny loaf, as much flour, the yolks of four eggs and two whites, a teaspoonful of ginger, half a pound of raisins, stoned, half a pound of currants, clean washed and picked, a little salt. Mix first the bread and flour, ginger, salt, and sugar, to your palate; then the eggs, and as much milk as will make it like a good batter; then the fruit; butter the dish, pour it in, and bake it.

A FINE PLAIN BAKED PUDDING.

You must take a quart of milk, and put three bay leaves in it. When it has boiled a little, with flour make it into a hasty-pudding, with a little salt, pretty thick; take it off the fire, and stir in half a pound of butter, a quarter of a pound of sugar; beat up twelve eggs, and half the whites; stir all well together, lay a puff-paste all over the dish, and pour in your stuff. Half an hour will bake it.

F 3

AN APRICOT PUDDING.

Coddle six large apricots very tender, break them small, sweeten to your taste. When they are cold, add six eggs, only two whites well beat; mix them well together with a pint of good cream, lay a puff-paste all over the dish, and pour in the ingredients. Bake it half an hour; do not let the oven be too hot; when it is enough, throw a little fine sugar over it, and send it to table hot.

A BREAD AND BUTTER PUDDING.

Get a twopenny loaf, and cut it in thin slices of bread and butter, as you do for tea. Butter a dish, as you cut them lay slices all over it, then strew a few currants, clean washed and picked; then a row of bread and butter, then a few currants, and so on, till the bread and butter is in; then take a pint of milk, beat up four eggs, a little salt, half a nutmeg, grated; mix all together with sugar to your taste; pour this over the bread, and bake it half an hour. A puff-paste under does best. You may put in two spoonfuls of rose-water.

A BOILED RICE PUDDING.

Get a quarter of a pound of the flour of rice, put it over the fire with a pint of milk, and keep it stirring constantly, that it may not clot nor burn. When it is of a good thickness, take it off, and pour it in an earthen pan; stir in half a pound of butter very smooth, and half a pint of cream or new milk, sweeten to your palate, grate in half a nutmeg, and the rind of a lemon. Beat up the yolks of six eggs and two whites, mix all well together; boil it either in small china basons or wooden bowls. When done, turn them into a dish, pour melted butter over, with a little sack, and throw sugar all over.

A CHEAP RICE PUDDING.

Get a quarter of a pound of rice, and half a pound of raisins, stoned, and tie them in a cloth. Give the rice a great deal of room to swell. Boil it two hours ; when it is enough, turn it into your dish, and pour melted butter and sugar over it, with a little nutmeg.

TO MAKE A CHEAP BAKED RICE PUDDING.

You must take a quarter of a pound of rice, boil it in a quart of new milk, stir it that it does not burn ; when it begins to be thick, take it off, let it stand till it is a little cool, then stir in well a quarter of a pound of butter ; sugar to your palate ; grate a nutmeg, butter your dish, pour it in, and bake it.

TO MAKE A QUAKING PUDDING.

Take a pint of cream, six eggs, and half the whites, beat them well, and mix with the cream ; grate a little nutmeg in, add a little salt, and a little rose-water, if it be agreeable ; grate in the crumb of a halfpenny roll, or a spoonful of flour, first mixed with a little of the cream, or a spoonful of the flour of rice. Butter a cloth well, and flour it ; then put in your mixture, tie it not too close, and boil it half an hour fast. Be sure the water boils before you put it in.

TO MAKE A CREAM PUDDING.

Take a quart of cream, boil it with a blade of mace, and half a nutmeg grated ; let it cool ; beat up eight eggs, and three whites, strain them well, mix a spoonful of flour with them, a quarter of a pound of almonds blanched, and beat fine, with a spoonful of orange-flower or rose-water, mix with the eggs, then by degrees mix in the cream, beat all well together; take a thick cloth, wet it and flour it well, pour in your stuff, tie it close, and boil it half an hour. Let the water boil fast; when it is done, turn it into your dish; pour melted butter over, with a little sack, and throw fine sugar all over it.

TO MAKE A PRUNE PUDDING.

Take a quart of milk, beat six eggs, half the whites, in half a pint of the milk, and four spoonfuls of flour, a little salt, and two spoonfuls of beaten ginger; then by degrees mix in all the milk, and a pound of prunes, tie it in a cloth, boil it an hour, melt butter and pour over it. Damsons eat well done this way in the room of prunes.

TO MAKE AN APPLE PUDDING.

Make a good puff-paste, roll it out half an inch thick, pare your apples, and core them, enough to fill the crust, close it up, tie it in a cloth, and boil it: if a small pudding, two hours; if a large one, three or four hours. When it is done, turn it into your dish, cut a piece of the crust out of the top, butter and sugar it to your palate; lay on the crust, and send it to table hot. A pear pudding, make the same way. And thus you may make a damson pudding, or any sort of plums, apricots, cherries or mulberries, and are very fine.

YEAST DUMPLINGS.

First make a light dough as for bread, with flour, water, salt, and yeast, cover with a cloth, and set it before the fire for half an hour; then have a sauce-

pan of water on the fire, and when it boils, take
the dough and make it into round balls, as big as a
large hen's egg; then flat them with your hand,
and put them in the boiling water; a few minutes
boils them. Take great care they do not fall to
the bottom of the pot or saucepan, for then they
will be heavy; and be sure to keep the water boiling
all the time. When they are enough, take them
up, (which will be in ten minutes or less,) lay them
in your dish, and have melted butter in a cup. As
good a way as any to save trouble, is to send to
the baker's for half a quartern of dough, (which
will make a great many,) and then you have only
to boil it.

NORFOLK DUMPLINGS.

Mix a thick batter as for pancakes, take half a
pint of milk, two eggs, a little salt, and make it into
a batter with flour. Have ready a clean saucepan
of water boiling, into which drop the batter. Be
sure the water boils fast, and two or three minutes
will boil them; then throw them into a sieve to
drain the water away; then turn them into a dish,
and stir a lump of fresh butter into them; eat
them hot, and they are very good.

HARD DUMPLINGS.

Mix flour and water with a little salt, like paste,
roll it in balls as big as a turkey's egg, roll them in
a little flour, have the water boiling, throw them in,
and half an hour will boil them. They are best
boiled with a good piece of beef. You may add,
for change, a few currants. Have melted butter
in a cup.

APPLE DUMPLINGS.

Make a good puff-paste; pare some large apples, cut them in quarters, and take out the cores very nicely; take a piece of crust, and roll it round, enough for one apple; if they are big, they will not look pretty, so roll the crust round each apple, and make them round with a little flour in your hand. Have a pot of water boiling, take a clean cloth, dip it in the water, and shake flour over it; tie each dumpling by itself, and put them in the water boiling, which keep boiling all the time; and if your crust is light and good, and the apples not too large, half an hour will do them; but if the apples be large, they will take an hour's boiling. When they are enough, take them up, and lay them in a dish; throw fine sugar over them, and send them to table. Have fresh butter melted in a cup, and fine beaten sugar in a saucer.

Rules to be observed in making Puddings, &c.

In boiled puddings, take great care the bag or cloth be very clean, not soapy, but dipped in hot water, and well floured. If a bread pudding, tie it loose; if a batter pudding, tie it close; and be sure the water boils when you put it in; and you should move it in the pot now and then, for fear it sticks. When you make a batter pudding, first mix the flour well with a little milk, then put in the ingredients by degrees, and it will be smooth and not have lumps; but for a plain batter pudding, the best way is to strain it through a coarse hair-sieve, that it may neither have lumps, nor the treadles of the eggs: and for all other puddings, strain the eggs when they are beat. If you boil them in wooden bowls, or china-dishes, butter the inside before you put in your batter; and for all baked puddings, butter the pan or dish before the pudding is put in.

OF PIES.

TO MAKE A SAVORY LAMB OR VEAL PIE.

Make a good puff-paste crust, cut your meat in pieces, season it to your palate with pepper, salt mace, cloves, and nutmeg, finely beat; lay it into your crust with a few lamb-stones and sweetbreads, seasoned as your meat; also oysters and force-meat balls, hard yolks of eggs, and the tops of asparagus, two inches long, first boiled green; put butter all over the pie, put on the lid, and set it on a quick oven an hour and a half, and have ready the liquor, made thus: take a pint of gravy, the oyster liquor, a gill of red wine, and a little grated nutmeg; mix all together with the yolks of two or three eggs beat, and keep it stirring one way all the time. When it boils pour it in your pie; put on the lid again. Send it hot to table. You must make liquor according to your pie.

A MUTTON PIE.

Take a loin of mutton, pare off the skin and fat off the inside, cut it into steaks, season it well with pepper and salt to your palate. Lay it in your crust, fill it, pour in as much water as will almost fill the dish; put on the crust, and bake it well.

A BEEF-STEAK PIE.

Take fine rump-steaks, beat them with a rolling-pin, then season with pepper and salt, according to your palate. Make a crust, lay in your steaks, fill

your dish, and pour in water, so as to half fill the
dish.   Put on the crust, and bake it well.

A HAM PIE.

Take some cold boiled ham, and slice it about
half an inch thick, make a good crust, and thick,
over the dish, and lay a layer of ham, shake a
little pepper over it, then take a large young fowl,
picked, gutted, washed, and singed; put a little
pepper and salt in the belly, rub a very little salt on
the outside; lay the fowl on the ham; boil some
eggs hard, put in the yolks, and cover with ham,
then shake some pepper on, and put on the crust.
Bake it well; have ready, when it comes out of the
oven, some rich beef-gravy, enough to fill the pie:
lay on the crust, and send it to table hot.   A fresh
ham will not be so tender; so that I boil my ham
one day, and bring it to table, and the next day
make a pie of it.   It does better than an unboiled
ham.   If you put two large fowls in, they will
make a fine pie; but that is according to your
company.   The larger the pie, the finer the meat
eats.   The crust must be the same you make for a
venison-pasty.   You should pour a little strong
gravy in the pie when you make it, just to bake the
meat, and fill it up when it comes out of the oven.
Boil some truffles and morels and put into the pie,
which is a great addition, and some fresh mushrooms, or dried ones.

A PIGEON PIE.

Make a puff-paste crust, cover your dish, let the
pigeons be very nicely picked and cleaned, season
them with pepper and salt, and put a good piece
of fresh butter, with pepper and salt, in their bellies;

lay them in a pan ; the necks, gizzards, livers, pinions, and hearts, lay between, with the yolk of a hard egg, and a beef-steak in the middle; put as much water as will almost fill the dish, lay on the top-crust, and bake it well. This is the best way; but the French fill the pigeons with a very high force-meat, and lay force-meat balls round the inside, with asparagus-tops, artichoke-bottoms, mushrooms, truffles, and morels, and season high; but that is according to different palates.

A GIBLET PIE.

Take two pair of giblets nicely cleaned, put all but the livers in a saucepan, with two quarts of water, twenty corns of whole pepper, three blade of mace, a bundle of sweet herbs, and a large onion ; cover them close, and stew them softly till they are tender ; then have a good crust ready, cover your dish, lay a fine rump-steak at the bottom, seasoned with pepper and salt; lay in your giblets with the livers, and strain the liquor they were stewed in. Season it with pepper and salt, and pour in your pie; put on the lid, and bake it an hour and a half.

A DUCK PIE.

Make a puff-paste crust, take two ducks, scald them, and make them clean, cut off the feet, the pinions, the neck, and head, picked and scalded clean, with the gizzards, livers, and hearts ; pick out all the fat of the inside; lay a crust over the dish, season the ducks with pepper and salt, inside and out, lay them in your dish, and the giblets at each end seasoned; put in as much water as will almost fill the pie, lay on the crust, and bake it, but not too much.

A CHICKEN PIE.

Make a puff-paste crust; take two chickens, cut them to pieces, season with pepper and salt, a little beaten mace, lay a force-meat, made thus, round the side of the dish : take half a pound of veal, half a pound of suet, beat them quite fine in a marble mortar, with as many crumbs of bread; season it with a little pepper and salt, an anchovy, with the liquor, cut it to pieces, a little lemon-peel cut very fine, and shred small, a very little thyme; mix all together with the yolk of an egg; make some into balls, about twelve, the rest lay round the dish. Lay in one chicken over the bottom of the dish; take two sweetbreads, cut them into five or six pieces, lay them all over, season with pepper and salt, strew over half an ounce of truffles and morels, two or three artichoke bottoms cut to pieces, a few cockscombs, a palate, boiled tender, and cut to pieces; then lay on the other part of the chicken, put half a pint of water in, and cover the pie; bake it well, and when it comes out of the oven, fill it with good gravy, lay on the crust, and send it to table.

A GOOSE PIE.

Half a peck of flour will make the walls of a goose pie, made as in the receipts for crust. Raise your crust just big enough to hold a large goose; first have a pickled dried tongue boiled tender enough to peel, cut off the root; bone a goose and a large fowl; take half a quarter of an ounce of mace beat fine, a large tea spoonful of beaten pepper, three tea spoonfuls of salt, mix all together, season the fowl and goose with it, lay the fowl in the goose, the tongue in the fowl, and the goose in the same form as if whole. Put half a pound of butter on the top, and lay on the lid. This pie is delicious, hot or cold, and will keep a great while. A slice of this pie, cut down across, makes a pretty side-dish for supper.

A VENISON PASTY.

Take a neck and breast of venison, bone it, season it with pepper and salt to your palate. Cut the breast in two or three pieces; but do not cut the fat of the neck, if you can help it. Lay in the breast and neck end first, and the best end of the neck on the top, that the fat may be whole; make a puff-paste crust, let it be very thick on the sides, a good bottom crust, and thick at top: cover the dish, lay in your venison, put in half a pound of butter, a quarter of a pint of water, close the pasty, and let it be baked two hours in a very quick oven. In the mean time, set on the bones of the venison in two quarts of water, two or three little blades of mace, an onion, a little piece of crust, baked crisp and brown, a little whole pepper; cover it close, and let it boil softly over a slow fire till above half is wasted, then strain it. When the pasty comes out of the oven, lift up the lid, and pour in the gravy. When the venison is not fat enough, take the fat of a loin of mutton, steeped in a little rape vinegar and red wine twenty-four hours, lay it on the top of the venison, and close your pasty. It is wrong of some people to think venison cannot be baked enough, and will first bake it in a false crust, and then in the pasty; by this time the fine flavor is gone. If you want it to be very tender, wash it in warm milk and water, dry it in clean cloths till it is very dry, then rub it all over with vinegar, and hang it in the air. Keep it as long as you think proper; it will keep thus a fortnight good; but be sure there be no moistness about it; if there is, you must dry it well, and throw ginger over it, and it will keep a long time. When you use it, just dip it in luke-warm water, and dry it. Bake it in a quick oven: if it is a large pasty, it will take three hours; then your venison will be tender, and have all the fine flavor. The shoulder makes a pretty pasty, boned, and made as above with the mutton fat.

MINCE PIES, THE BEST WAY.

Take three pounds of suet, shred very fine, and chopped as small as possible; two pounds of raisins, stoned, and chopped as fine as possible; two pounds of currants nicely picked, washed, rubbed and dried at the fire; half an hundred of fine pippins, pared, cored, and chopped small; half a pound of fine sugar, pounded; a quarter of an ounce of mace, the same of cloves, two large nutmegs, all beat fine; put all together into a great pan, and mix it well with half a pint of brandy, and half a pint of sack; put it down close in a stone pot, and it will keep good four months. When you make your pies, take a little dish, something bigger than a soup-plate, lay a thin crust all over it, lay a thin layer of meat, and then a thin layer of citrons, cut very thin; then a layer of mince-meat, and a layer of orange-peel, cut thin, over that a little meat, squeeze half the juice of a fine Seville orange or lemon, lay on your crust, and bake it nicely. These pies eat finely cold. If you make them in little patties, mix your meat and sweetmeats accordingly. If you choose meat in your pies, parboil a neat's tongue, peel it, and chop the meat as fine as possible, and mix with the rest; or two pounds of the inside of a sirloin of beef, boiled.

DIFFERENT SORTS OF TARTS.

If you bake in tin patties, butter them, and you must put a little crust all over, because of the taking them out; if in china or glass, no crust but the top one. Lay fine sugar at the bottom; then plums, cherries, or any other sort of fruit, and sugar at top; put on your lid, and bake them in a slack oven. Mince-pies must be baked in tin patties, because of taking them out, and puff-paste is best for them. For sweet tarts the beaten crust is best; but as you fancy. See the receipt for the crust in this chapter. Apple, pear, apricot, &c. make thus: apples and pears, pare them, cut them into quarters, and core them; cut the quarters across again, set them on in a saucepan, with just as much water as will barely cover them; let them simmer on a slow fire till the fruit is tender; put a good piece of lemon-peel in the water with the fruit, then have your patties ready. Lay fine sugar at bottom, then your fruit, and a little sugar at top; that you must put in at your discretion. Pour over each tart a tea spoonful of lemon-juice, and three tea spoonfuls of the liquor they were boiled in; put on your lid, and bake them in a slack oven. Apricots do the same way, only do not use lemon.

As to preserved tarts, only lay in your preserved fruit, and put a thin crust at top, and let them be baked as little as possible; but if you would make them very nice, have a large patty, the size you would have your tart. Make your sugar crust, roll it as thick as a halfpenny; then butter your patties, and cover it. Shape your upper crust on a hollow thing on purpose, the size of the patty, and mark it with a marking-iron in what shape you please, to be hollow and open to see the fruit through; then bake the crust in a very slack oven, not to discolour it, but to have it crisp. When the crust is cold, very carefully take it out, and fill it with what fruit you please; lay on the lid, and it is done; therefore, if the tart is not eat, your sweatmeat is not the worse, and it looks genteel.

PASTE FOR TARTS.

One pound of flour, three quarters of a pound of butter, mix up together, and beat well with a rolling-pin.

PUFF-PASTE.

Take a quarter of a peck of flour, rub in a pound of butter, very fine, make it up in a light paste with cold water, just stiff enough to work it up; then roll it about as thick as a crown-piece, put a layer of butter all over, sprinkle on a little flour, double it up, and roll it out again; double it, and roll it out seven or eight times; then it is fit for all sorts of pies and tarts that require a puff-paste.

A GOOD CRUST FOR GREAT PIES.

To a peck of flour add the yolks of three eggs;

boil some water, and put in half a pound of fried suet, and a pound and a half of butter. Skim off the butter and suet, and as much of the liquor as will make it a light good crust; work it up well, and roll it out.

A DRIPPING CRUST.

Take a pound and a half of beef-dripping, boil it in water, strain it, let it stand to be cold, and take off the hard fat: scrape it, boil it four or five times, then work it well up into three pounds of flour, as fine as you can, and make it up into paste with cold water. It makes a very fine crust.

A CRUST FOR CUSTARDS.

Take half a pound of flour, six ounces of butter, the yolks of two eggs, three spoonfuls of cream; mix them together, and let them stand a quarter of an hour, then work it up and down, and roll it very thin.

PASTE FOR CRACKLING CRUST.

Blanch four handfuls of almonds, and throw them in water, then dry them in a cloth, and pound them very fine, with a little orange-flower-water, and the white of an egg. When they are well pounded, pass them through a coarse hair-sieve to clear them from all the lumps or clots; then spread it on a dish till it is very pliable; let it stand for a while, then roll out a piece for the under-crust, and dry it in the oven on the pie-pan, while other pastry-works are making, as knots, cyphers, &c. for garnishing your pies.

AN APPLE PIE.

Make a puff-paste crust, lay some round the

II

sides of the dish, pare and quarter your apples, and take out the cores, lay a row of apples thick, throw in half the sugar you design for your pie, mince a little lemon-peel fine, throw over, and squeeze a little lemon over them, then a few cloves, here and there one, then the rest of your apples, and the rest of your sugar. You must sweeten to your palate, and squeeze a little more lemon. Boil the peelings of the apples and the cores in a little water, a blade of mace, till it is very good; strain it, and boil the syrup with a little sugar, till there is but very little; pour it in your pie, put on your upper crust and bake it. You may put in a little quince or marmalade if you please.

Thus make a pear pie, but do not put in any quince. You may butter them when they come out of the oven, or beat up the yolks of two eggs, and half a pint of cream, with a little nutmeg, sweetened with sugar; put it over a slow fire, and keep stirring it till it just boils up, take off the lid, and pour in the cream. Cut the crust in little three-corner pieces, stick about the pie, and send it to table.

A CHERRY PIE.

Make a good crust, lay a little round the sides of your dish, throw sugar at the bottom; and lay in your fruit and sugar at top; a few red currants does well with them; put on the lid, and bake in a slack oven.

Make a plum pie the same way, and a gooseberry pie. If you would have it red, let it stand a good while in the oven after the bread is drawn. A custard is very good with the gooseberry pie.

AN EEL PIE.

Make a good crust; clean, gut, and wash the eels well, cut them in pieces half as long as your finger; season them with pepper, salt, and a little beaten mace to your palate, either high or low. Fill the dish with eels, and put as much water as the dish will hold; put on your cover, and bake it well.

A FLOUNDER PIE.

Gut some flounders, wash them clean, dry them in a cloth, just boil them, cut off the meat clean from the bones, lay a crust over the dish, and a little fresh butter at the bottom, and on the fish; season with pepper and salt to your mind. Boil the bones in the water your fish was boiled in, with a little bit of horse-radish, a little parsley, a very little bit of lemon-peel, and a crust of bread. Boil it till there is just enough liquor for the pie, then strain it, and put it in your pie : put on the top crust, and bake it.

A SALMON PIE.

Make a good crust, cleanse a piece of salmon well, season it with salt, mace, and nutmeg; lay a piece of butter at the bottom of the dish, and lay your salmon in, Melt butter according to your pie; take a lobster, boil it, pick out all the flesh, chop it small, bruise the body, mix it well with the butter, which must be very good; pour it over your salmon, put on the lid, and bake it well.

A LOBSTER PIE.

Take two or three lobsters, boil them; take the meat out of the tails whole, cut them in four pieces long-ways; take out all the spawn and the meat of the claws, beat it well in a mortar; season with pepper, salt, two spoonfuls of vinegar, and a little anchovy-liquor; melt half a pound of fresh butter, stir all together, with the crumbs of a penny roll rubbed through a fine cullender, and the yolks of two eggs; put a fine puff-paste over your dish, lay in your tails, and the rest of the meat over them: put on the cover, and bake it in a slow oven.

VARIETY OF DISHES FOR LENT.

A RICE SOUP.

Take two quarts of water, a pound of rice, a little cinnamon: cover close, and let it simmer very softly till the rice is quite tender; take out the cinnamon; then sweeten to your palate, grate half a nutmeg, and let it stand till it is cold; then beat up the yolks of three eggs, with half a pint of white wine, mix them well, then stir them into the rice, set them on a slow fire, and keep stirring all the time for fear of curdling. When it is of a good thickness, and boils, take it up. Keep stirring it till you put it into your dish.

PEAS-PORRIDGE.

To a quart of green peas, add a quart of water, a bundle of dried mint, and a little salt. Let them boil till the peas are quite tender; then put in some beaten pepper, a piece of butter as big as a walnut, rolled in flour, stir it altogether, and boil it a few minutes; then add two quarts of milk, let it boil a quarter of an hour, take out the mint, and serve it up.

RICE MILK.

Take half a pound of rice, boil it in a quart of

water, with a little cinnamon. Let it boil till the
water is all wasted; take great care it does not
burn; then add three pints of milk, and the yolk
of an egg beat up. Keep it stirring, and when it
boils take it up. Sweeten to your palate.

AN ORANGE-FOOL.

Take the juice of six oranges, and six eggs well
beaten, a pint of cream, a quarter of a pound of
sugar, a little cinnamon and nutmeg. Mix all
together, and keep stirring over a slow fire till it is
thick, then a little bit of butter, and keep stirring
till cold, and dish it up.

PLUM-PORRIDGE, OR BARLEY-GRUEL.

Take a gallon of water, half a pound of barley,
a quarter of a pound of raisins, clean washed, a
quarter of a pound of currants washed and picked.
Boil till above half the water is wasted, with two
or three blades of mace; then sweeten to your
palate, and add half a pint of white wine.

A HASTY-PUDDING.

Take a quart of milk, and four bay-leaves, set it
on the fire to boil, beat up the yolks of two eggs,
and stir in a little salt. Take two or three spoonfuls of milk, and beat up with your eggs, and stir
in the milk, then, with a wooden spoon in one
hand, and flour in the other, stir it in till it is of a
good thickness, but not too thick. Let it boil, and
keep it stirring, then pour it in a dish, and stick
pieces of butter here and there. You may omit the
egg if you do not like it; but it is a great addition
to the pudding; and a little piece of butter stirred
in the milk makes it eat short and fine. Take out
the bay-leaves before you put in the flour.

APPLE-FRITTERS.

Beat the yolks of eight eggs, and the whites of four, well together, and strain them into a pan; then take a quart of cream, make it as hot as you can bear your finger in it; put to it a quarter of a pint of sack, three quarters of a pint of ale, and make a posset of it. When cool, put it to the eggs, beating it well together; then put in nutmeg, ginger, salt, and flour, to your liking. Your batter should be pretty thick, then put in pippins, sliced or scraped, and fry them in a deal of batter quick.

PANCAKES.

In a quart of milk, beat six or eight eggs, leaving half the whites out; mix it well till your batter is of a fine thickness. You must observe to mix your flour first with a little milk, then add the rest by degrees; put in two spoonfuls of beaten ginger, a glass of brandy, a little salt; stir all together, clean the stewpan well, put in a piece of butter as big as a walnut, then pour in a ladleful of batter, moving the pan round that the batter be all over the pan: shake the pan, and when you think that side is enough, toss it; if you cannot, turn it cleverly; and when both sides are done, lay it in a dish before the fire; and so do the rest. You must take care they are dry; before sent to table, strew a little sugar over them.

TO BAKE APPLES WHOLE.

Put apples in an earthen pan, with a few cloves, a little lemon-peel, some coarse sugar, a glass of red wine; put them into a quick oven, and they will take an hour baking.

TO STEW PEARS.

Pare six pears, and quarter them, or do them
whole; they make a pretty dish with one whole,
the rest cut in quarters, and the cores taken out.
Lay them in a deep earthen-pot, with a few cloves,
a piece of lemon-peel, a gill of red wine, and
a quarter of a pound of fine sugar. If the pears
are very large, put half a pound of sugar, and half
a pint of red wine; cover close with brown paper,
and bake them till they are enough. Serve them
hot or cold, just as you like them; and they will
be very good with water instead of wine.

A TANSEY.

Take a pint of cream, and half a pint of blanched
almonds, beat fine with rose and orange-flower-
water, stir them together over a slow fire; when
it boils take it off, and let stand till cold, then beat
in ten eggs, grate in a small nutmeg, four Naples
biscuits, a little grated bread; sweeten to your
taste, and if you think it is too thick, put in more
cream, and the juice of spinage to make it green;
stir it well together, and either fry or bake it. If
you fry it, do one side first, and then with a dish
turn the other.

STEWED SPINAGE AND EGGS.

Pick and wash spinage clean, put it in a saucepan, with a little salt; cover it close, shake the
pan often; when it is tender, and whilst it is green,
throw it into a sieve to drain; lay it in your dish.
In the mean time, have a stewpan of water boiling;
break as many eggs into cups as you would poach.
When the water boils put in the eggs, have an egg-
slice ready to take them out, lay them on the

spinage, and garnish the dish with an orange, cut in quarters, with melted butter in a cup.

TO COLLAR EELS.

Take an eel and scour it well with salt, wipe it clean; then cut it down the back, take out the bone, cut the head and tail off; put the yoke of an egg over; then take four cloves, two blades of mace, half a nutmeg beat fine, a little pepper and salt, some chopped parsley, and sweet herbs chopped fine; mix them all together, and sprinkle over it, roll the eel up very tight, and tie it in a cloth; put on water enough to boil it, and put in an onion, some cloves and mace, and four bay-leaves; boil it up with the bones, head and tail, for half an hour, with a little vinegar and salt; then take out the bones, &c. and put in the eels; boil them, if large, two hours; lesser in proportion :· when done, put them to cool; then take them out of the liquor and cloth, and cut them in slices, or send them whole, with raw parsley under and over.

N. B. You must take them out of the cloth, and put them in the liquor, and tie them close down to keep.

TO PICKLE OR BAKE HERRINGS.

Scale and wash them clean, cut off the heads, take out the roes, or wash them clean, and put them in again, as you like. Season with a little mace and cloves beat, a very little beaten pepper and salt, lay them in a deep pan, lay two or three bay-leaves between each layer, put in half vinegar and half water, or rape vinegar. Cover it close with a brown paper, and send it to the oven: let it stand till cold. Thus do sprats. Some use only allspice, but that is not so good.

TO SOUSE MACKAREL.

Wash them clean, gut them, and boil them in salt and water till they are enough; take them out, lay them in a clean pan, cover them with liquor, add a little vinegar; and when you send them to table, lay fennel over them.

OF HOG'S-PUDDINGS, SAUSAGES, &c.

BLACK PUDDINGS.

First, before you kill a hog, get a peck of grits, boil them half an hour in water, then drain them, and put them into a clean tub or large pan; then kill the hog, and save two quarts of the blood, and keep stirring it till quite cold; then mix it with grits, and stir them well together. Season with a large spoonful of salt, a quarter of an ounce of cloves, mace and nutmeg together, an equal quantity of each; dry it, beat it well, and mix in. Take a little winter-savory, sweet-marjoram, and thyme, penny-royal stripped off the stalks, and chopped fine, just enough to season them, and to give them a flavour, but no more. The next day take the leaf of the hog, and cut in dice, scrape and wash the gut clean, then tie one end, and begin to fill them; mix in the fat as you fill them; be sure to put in a deal of fat, fill the skins three parts full, tie the other end, and make them what length you please; prick them with a pin, and put them in a kettle of boiling water, Boil them softly an hour; take them out, and lay them on clean straw.

TO MAKE SAUSAGES.

Take three pounds of pork, fat and lean together,

without skin or gristles, chop it as fine as possible, season with a tea-spoonful of beaten pepper, and two of salt, some sage shred fine, about three spoonfuls; mix it well together; have the guts nicely cleaned, and fill them; or put them down in a pot, then roll them of what size you please, and fry them.   Beef makes good sausages.

TO CURE HAMS, &c.
TO COLLAR BEEF.

Take a piece of thin flank of beef, and bone it; cut the skin off, salt it with two ounces of saltpetre, two ounces of sal prunella, two of bay salt: half a pound of coarse sugar, and two pounds of white salt; beat the hard salts fine, and mix all together; turn it every day, and rub it with the brine well for eight days,; then take it out of the pickle, wash it, and wipe it dry ; then take a quarter of an ounce of cloves, and a quarter of an ounce of mace, twelve corns of allspice, and a nutmeg, beat fine, with a spoonful of beaten pepper, a large quantity of chopped parsley, with sweet herbs chopped fine; sprinkle it on the beef, and roll it up tight, put a coarse cloth round, and tie it tight with beggar's tape: boil it in a large copper of water; if a large collar, six hours; if a small one, five hours: take it out, and put it in a press till cold; if you have never a press, put it between two boards, and a large weight on it till it is cold; then take it out of the cloth, and cut it into slices.   Garnish with raw parsley.

TO PICKLE PORK.

Bone pork, cut it into pieces of a size fit to lie in the tub or pan you design it to lie in, rub your pieces well with saltpetre, then take two parts of common salt, and two of bay salt, rub every piece well; put a layer of common salt in the bottom of the vessel, cover every piece with common salt, lay them one on another as close as you can, filling the hollow places on the sides with salt. As the salt melts on the top, strew on more; lay a coarse cloth over the vessel, a board over that, and a weight on the board to keep it down. Keep it close covered; it will keep the whole year. Put a pound of saltpetre and two pounds of bay salt to a hog.

A Pickle for Pork which is to be eaten soon.

Take two gallons of pump water, one pound of bay salt, one pound of coarse sugar, six ounces of saltpetre; boil all together, and skim it when cold. Cut the pork in what pieces you please, lay it down close, and pour the liquor over it. Lay a weight on it to keep it down, and cover it close from the air, and it will be fit to use in a week. If you find the pickle begins to spoil, boil and skim it: when cold, pour it on the pork.

MUTTON HAMS.

Take a hind quarter of mutton, cut it like a ham; take an ounce of saltpetre, a pound of coarse sugar, a pound of common salt; mix them, and rub the ham; lay it in a hollow tray, with the skin downwards, baste it every day for a fortnight, then roll it in sawdust, and hang it in the wood-smoke a fortnight; boil it, and hang it in a dry place, and cut it out in rashers. It does not eat well boiled, but eats finely broiled.

PORK HAMS.

Take a fat hind-quarter of pork, and cut off
a fine ham. Take two ounces of saltpetre, a pound
of coarse sugar, a pound of common salt, and two
ounces of sal prunella; mix all together, and rub it
well. Let it lie a month in this pickle, turning
and basting it every day; then hang it in wood-
smoke as you do beef, in a dry place, so as no heat
comes to it; and if you keep them long, hang
them a month or two in a damp place, so as they
will be mouldy, and it will make them cut fine and
short. Never lay them in water till you boil them,
and then boil them in a copper, if you have one,
or the biggest pot you have. Put them in the cold
water, and let them be four or five hours before
they boil. Skim the pot well, and often, till it boils.
If it is a very large one, three hours will boil it;
if small, two hours will do, provided it be a great
while before the water boils. Take it up half an
hour before dinner, pull off the skin, and sift raspings over. Hold a red-hot fire-shovel over it,
and when dinner is ready, take a few raspings in
a sieve, and sift all over the dish; then lay in the
ham, and with your finger make figures round the
edge of the dish. Be sure to boil the ham in as
much water as you can, and skim it all the time till
it boils. It must be at least four hours before it boils.

This pickle does finely for tongues afterwards,
to lie in it a fortnight, and then hung in a wood-
smoke a fortnight, or boil them out of the pickle.

When you broil any of these hams in slices, have
boiling water ready, and let the slices lie a minute
or two in the water, then broil them; it takes out
the salt, and makes them eat finer.

OF PICKLING.

TO PICKLE WALNUTS.

Take large full-grown nuts, before they are hard, lay them in salt and water; let them lie two days, then shift them into fresh water; let them lie two days longer, then shift them again, and let them lie three days; take them out of the water, and put them in a pickling jar. When the jar is half full, put in a large onion stuck with cloves. To a hundred of walnuts, put in half a pint of mustard-seed, a quarter of an ounce of mace, half an ounce of black pepper, half an ounce of allspice, six bay leaves, and a stick of horse-radish: then fill the jar, and pour boiling vinegar over them. Cover them with a plate, and when they are cold, tie them down with a bladder and leather, and they will be fit to eat in two or three months. The next year, if any remains, boil up the vinegar again, and skim it; when cold, pour it over the walnuts. This is by much the best pickle for use; therefore you may add more vinegar to it, what quantity you please. If you pickle a great many walnuts, and eat them fast, make pickle for a hundred or two, the rest keep in a strong brine of salt and water, boiled till it will bear an egg, and, as the pot empties, fill them up with those in the salt and water. Take care they are covered with pickle.

TO PICKLE GHERKINS AND FRENCH BEANS.

Take five hundred gherkins, and have ready a large earthen pan of spring-water and salt, put to every gallon of water two pounds of salt; mix it well together, and put in the gherkins, wash them out in two hours, and put them to drain, let them

be dry, and put in a jar: in the mean time get
a bell-metal pot, with a gallon of the best white
wine vinegar, half an ounce of cloves and mace,
an ounce of allspice, an ounce of mustard-seed,
a stick of horse-radish cut in slices, six bay leaves,
a little dill, two or three races of ginger cut in
pieces, a nutmeg cut in pieces, and a handful of
salt; boil it in the pot, and put it over the gherkins;
cover close down, and let them stand twenty-four
hours; then put them in the pot, and simmer them
over the stove till they are green; be careful not
to let them boil, if you do you will spoil them; then
put them in a jar, and cover them close down till
cold; then tie them over with a bladder, and
a leather over that; put them in a cold dry place.
Mind always to keep pickles tied down close, and
take them out with a wooden spoon, or one kept
on purpose.

TO PICKLE LARGE CUCUMBERS IN SLICES.

Take large cucumbers before they are too ripe,
slice them the thickness of crown-pieces in a pewter
dish; and to every dozen of cucumbers slice two
large onions thin, and so on till you have filled the
dish, with a handful of salt between every row;
then cover them with another pewter dish, and let
them stand twenty-four hours, put them in a cullender, and let them drain well; put them in a jar,
cover them over with white wine vinegar, and let
them stand four hours; pour the vinegar from
them in a copper saucepan, and boil it with a little
salt: put to the cucumbers a little mace, a little
whole pepper, a large race of ginger sliced, then
pour the boiling vinegar on. Cover close, and

when they are cold, tie them down. They will be fit to eat in two or three days.

TO PICKLE BEET-ROOT.

Set a pot of spring water on the fire; when it boils put in the beets, and boil them till tender; take them out, and with a knife take off all the outside, cut them in pieces according to your fancy; put them in a jar, and cover them with cold vinegar, and tie them down close: when you use it, take it out of the pickle, and cut it in what shapes you like; put it in a little dish with pickle over, or use it for sallads, or garnish.

TO PICKLE ONIONS.

Take onions when they are dry enough to lay up for winter, the smaller they are the better they look; put them in a pot, and cover them with spring water, with a handful of white salt, let them boil up, then strain them off, and take three coats off; put them on a cloth, and let two people take hold of it, one at each end, and rub them backward and forward till they are very dry; then put them in bottles, with some blades of mace and cloves, and a nutmeg cut in pieces; have double distilled white wine vinegar, boil it up with a little salt, and put it over the onions; when they are cold, cork them close, and tie a bladder and leather over it.

TO PICKLE RED CABBAGE.

Slice the cabbage fine cross-ways; put it on an earthen dish, and sprinkle a handful of salt over it, cover it with another dish, and let it stand twenty-four hours; put it in a cullender to drain, and lay it in a jar; take white wine vinegar enough to cover it, a little cloves, mace, and allspice, put them in whole, with one penny-worth of cochineal, bruised fine; boil it up, and put it over hot or cold, which you like best, and cover it close with a cloth till cold, then tie it over with leather.

TO PICKLE SAMPHIRE.

Take samphire that is green; lay it in a clean pan, throw two or three handfuls of salt over, then cover it with spring water, let it lie twenty-four hours, put it in a clean brass saucepan, throw in a handful of salt, and cover it with good vinegar. Cover the pan close, and set it over a slow fire, let it stand till it is just green and crisp, then take it off in a moment; for if it stands to be soft, it is spoiled ; put it in a pickling pot, and cover close : when it is cold, tie it down with a bladder and leather, and keep it for use. Or you may keep it all the year in a very strong brine of salt and water, throw it into vinegar just before you use it.

Rules to be observed in Pickling.

Always use stone jars for all sorts of pickles that require hot pickle to them. The first charge is the least, for these not only last longer, but keep the pickle better ; for vinegar and salt will penetrate through all earthen vessels ; stone and glass are the only things to keep pickles in. Be sure never to put your hands in to take pickles out, it will soon spoil them. The best method is, to every pot tie a wooden spoon, full of little holes, to take the pickles out with.

OF MAKING CAKES, &c.

A POUND CAKE.

Take a pound of butter, beat it in an earthen

pan with your hand one way, till it is like a fine
thick cream ; have ready twelve eggs, but half the
whites ; beat them well, and beat them up with the
butter, a pound of flour beat in it, a pound of
sugar, and a few carraways. Beat it well together
for an hour with your hand, or a great wooden
spoon, butter a pan, and put it in, and then bake it
an hour in a quick oven.

For change, put in a pound of currants, washed
and picked.

A CHEAP SEED CAKE.

You must take half a peck of flour, a pound and
a half of butter, put it in a saucepan with a pint
of new milk, and set it on the fire ; take a pound
of sugar, half an ounce of allspice, beat fine, and
mix with the flour. When the butter is melted,
pour the milk and butter in the middle of the flour,
and work it up like paste. Pour in with the milk
half a pint of good ale-yeast ; set it before the
fire to rise, just before it goes to the oven. Either
put in currants or carraway seeds, and bake it in a
quick oven. Make it in two cakes. They will
take an hour and a half baking.

TO MAKE BUNS.

Take two pounds of flour, a pint of ale-yeast,
put a little sack in the yeast, and three eggs beaten,
knead all together with a little warm milk, nutmeg,
and salt, and lay it before the fire till it rises very
light, then knead in a pound of fresh butter, a
pound of rough carraway comfits, and bake them
in a quick oven, in what shape you please, on
floured paper.

OF CUSTARDS, JELLIES, PRESERVING, &c.

PLAIN CUSTARDS.

Take a quart of new milk, sweeten to your taste, grate in a little nutmeg, beat up eight eggs, leave out half the whites, beat them up well, stir them into the milk, and bake it in china basons, or put them in a deep china dish; have a kettle of water boiling, set the cup in, let the water come above half way, but do not let it boil too fast, for fear of its getting in the cups. You may add a little rose-water.

CALF'S FOOT JELLY.

Boil two calf's feet in a gallon of water, till it comes to a quart, strain it, let it stand till cold, skim off the fat, and take the jelly up clean. If there is any settling in the bottom, leave it; put the jelly in a saucepan, with a pint of mountain-wine, half a pound of loaf-sugar, the juice of four large lemons; beat up six or eight whites of eggs with a whisk, then put them in a saucepan, and stir all together till it boils. Let it boil a few minutes. Have ready a large flannel bag, pour it in, it will run through quick, pour it in again till it runs clear, then have ready a large china basin, with the lemon-peels cut as thin as posible, let the jelly run into that basin, and the peels both give it a fine amber colour, and also a flavour: with a clean silver spoon fill the glasses.

CURRANT JELLY.

Strip currants from the stalks, put them in a stone jar, stop it close, set it in a kettle of boiling water, half way up the jar, let it boil half an hour, take it out, and strain the juice through a coarse hair-sieve; to a pint of juice put a pound of sugar, set it over a fine quick clear fire in a preserving pan, or bell-metal skillet; keep stirring it till the sugar is melted, then skim the scum off as fast as it rises. When the jelly is very clear and fine, pour it in gallipots; when cold, cut white paper the size of the top of the pot, and lay on the jelly, dip the papers in brandy; cover the top close with white paper, and prick it full of holes; set it in a dry place; put some in glasses, and paper them.

RASPBERRY JAM.

Take a pint of currant jelly, and a quart of raspberries, bruise them well together, set them over a slow fire, keeping them stirring all the time till it boils. Let it boil gently half an hour, and stir it round very often to keep it from sticking; pour it in gallipots, paper as you do currant jelly, and keep it for use. They will keep for two or three years, and have the full flavour of the raspberry.

A FINE SYLLABUB FROM THE COW.

Make a syllabub of either cyder or wine, sweeten it pretty sweet, and grate nutmeg in; then milk into the liquor; when this is done, pour over the top half a pint or a pint of cream, according to the quantity of syllabub you make.

You may make this at home, only have new milk; make it as hot as milk from the cow, and out of a tea-pot, or any such thing, pour it in, holding your hand very high.

TO PRESERVE DAMSONS WHOLE.

Take some damsons, and cut them in pieces, put them in a skillet over the fire, with as much water

as will cover them. When they are boiled, and
the liquor pretty strong, strain it out; add for
every pound of the damsons wiped clean, a pound
of single refined sugar, put the third part of the
sugar in the liquor, set it over the fire, and when it
simmers, put in the damsons; boil them once well,
take them off for half an hour, covered up close;
set them on again, and simmer them over the fire,
after turning them; take them out, and put them
in a basin, strew all the sugar that was left on them,
and pour the hot liquor over. Cover them up, and
let them stand till the next day, then boil them
again, till they are enough. Take them up, and
put them in pots; boil the liquor till it jellies, and
pour it on them when it is almost cold; so paper
them up.

To preserve Gooseberries whole without Stoning.

Take the largest preserving gooseberries, and
pick off the black eye, but not the stalk; then set
them over the fire in a pot of water to scald, cover
close, but not boil or break, and when they are
tender, take them up in cold water; then take a
pound and a half of double refined sugar to a
pound of gooseberries, and clarify the sugar with
water, a pint to a pound of sugar; and when the
syrup is cold, put the gooseberries single in the
preserving pan, put the syrup to them, and set them
on a gentle fire; let them boil, but not too fast,
lest they break; and when they have boiled, and
you perceive that the sugar has entered them,
take them off; cover them with white paper, and
set them by till the next day; take them out of the
syrup, and boil the syrup till it begins to be ropy,

skim and put it to them again ; set them on a gentle fire, and let them simmer gently, till you perceive the syrup will rope; take them off, set them by till they are cold, cover with paper; boil some gooseberries in fair water, and when the liquor is strong, strain it out. Let it stand to settle, and to every pint take a pound of double refined sugar; make a jelly of it, put the gooseberries in glasses, when they are cold, cover them with the jelly, paper them wet, and half dry the paper that goes in the inside, it closes down better, and then white paper over the glass. Set it in your stove, or a dry place.

TO PRESERVE CURRANTS.

Take the weight of your currants in sugar, pick out the seeds ; take to a pound of sugar half a jack of water, let it melt, then put in the berries, and let them do leisurely, skim them, and take them up, let the syrup boil; put them on again, and when they are clear, and the syrup thick enough, take them off, and when they are cold put them up in glasses.

TO PRESERVE RASPBERRIES.

Take raspberries that are not too ripe, and take the weight of them in sugar, wet the sugar with a little water, and put in the berries, and let them boil softly, take heed of breaking them ; when they are clear, take them up, and boil the syrup till it be thick enough, then put them in again, and when they are cold put them in glasses.

TO PRESERVE CHERRIES.

Take their weight in sugar before you stone them; when stoned, make the syrup, put in the cherries; boil them slowly at the first, till they are thoroughly warmed, then boil them as fast as you can : when they are boiled clear, put in the jelly, with near their weight in sugar ; strew the sugar on the cherries ; for the colouring, be ruled by your eye ; to a pound of sugar put a jack of water, strew the sugar on them before they boil, and put in the juice of currants soon after they boil.

ICE CREAM.

Take two pewter basins, one larger than the other; the inward one must have a close cover, in which put cream, and mix it with raspberries, or whatever you like best, to give it a flavour and colour. Sweeten to your palate, then cover close, and set it in the larger basin. Fill it with ice, and a handful of salt : let it stand in this ice three quarters of an hour, uncover it, and stir the cream well together; cover it close again, and let it stand half an hour longer, after that turn it into a plate. These things are made at the pewterers.

OF MADE-WINES, &c.

RAISIN WINE.

Take two hundred weight of raisins, stalks and all, and put them in a large hogshead, fill it with water, let them steep a fortnight, stirring them every day; pour off the liquor, and press the raisins. Put both liquors together in a nice clean vessel that will just hold it, for it must be full; let it stand till it has done hissing, or making the least noise, stop it close, and let it stand six months. Peg it, and if you find it clear, rack it off in another vessel; stop it close for three months longer, then bottle it, and, when used, decanter it off.

ELDER WINE.

To every gallon of ripe elder-berries put four gallons of water, half an ounce of ginger, and two ounces of allspice; boil it twenty minutes, strain it through a hair sieve, and put it in your pan again, with three pounds of moist sugar to every gallon, boil it thirty minutes; put in your tub a few pounds of raisins cut in halves, pour the liquor on them, put to it some ale yeast, let it work three days, then tun it, (or half a pint of raisin wine to every gallon); add a quart of brandy to every 36 gallons; bottle it at Christmas, or let it stand in the cask at least three months.

ORANGE WINE.

Take twelve pounds of the best powder sugar, the whites of eight or ten eggs, well beaten, into six gallons of spring water, and boil it three quarters of an hour. When cold, put in it six spoonfuls of yeast, and the juice of twelve lemons, which being pared, must stand with two pounds of white sugar in a tankard, and in the morning skim off the top, and then put in the water; add the juice and rinds of fifty oranges, but not the white parts of the rinds, and so let it work all together two days and two nights; add two quarts of Rhenish or white wine, and put it into your vessel.

GOOSEBERRY WINE.

Gather gooseberries in dry weather, when they are half ripe, pick them, and bruise a peck in a tub with a wooden mallet; then take a horse-hair cloth, and press them as much as possible, without breaking the seeds. When all the juice is pressed out, to every gallon of gooseberries, put three pounds of fine dry powder sugar, stir it together till the sugar is dissolved, put it in a cask, which must be quite full : if ten or twelve gallons, let it stand a fortnight ; if a twenty-gallon cask, five weeks. Set it in a cool place, then draw it off from the lees, clear the vessel of the lees, and pour in the clear liquor again. If it be a ten-gallon cask, let it stand three months; if a twenty-gallon, four months; then bottle it off.

CURRANT WINE.

Gather currants on a fine dry day, when the fruit is full ripe, strip and put them in a large pan, and bruise them with a wooden pestle. Let them stand in a pan, or tub, twenty-four hours to ferment ; then run it through a hair-sieve, and do not let your hand touch the liquor. To every gallon of this liquor, put two pounds and a half of white sugar, stir it well together, and put it in your vessel. To every six gallons, put in a quart of brandy, and let it stand six weeks. If it is fine, bottle it; if not, draw it off as clear as you can into another vessel, or large bottles ; and in a fortnight, bottle it off.

CHERRY WINE.

Pull cherries, when full ripe, off the stalks, and press them through a hair-sieve. To every gallon of liquor, put two pounds of lump, sugar beat fine; stir it together, and put it in a vessel ; it must be full ; when it has done working, and making any noise, stop it close for three months, and bottle it off.

RASPBERRY WINE.

Take fine raspberries, bruize them with the back

of a spoon, then strain them through a flannel bag into a flour-jar. To each quart of juice, put a pound of double refined sugar, stir it well together, and cover it close ; let it stand three days, then pour it off clear. To a quart of juice, put two quarts of white wine, bottle it off : it will be fit to drink in a week. Brandy made thus is a very fine dram, and a much better way than steeping the raspberries.

TO MAKE CATCHUP.

Take the large flaps of mushrooms, pick nothing but the straws and dirt from them, lay them in a broad good earthen pan, strew a deal of salt over them, let them lie till next morning, then with your hand break them, put them in a stewpan, let them boil a minute or two, strain them through a coarse cloth, and wring it hard. Take out the juice, let it stand to settle, then pour it off clear, run it through a thick flannel bag, (some filter it through brown paper, but that is tedious,) then boil it: to a quart of liquor, put a quarter of an ounce of whole ginger, and half a quarter of an ounce of whole pepper. Boil it briskly a quarter of an hour: strain it, and when it is cold, put it in pint bottles. In each bottle, put four or five blades of mace, and six cloves, cork it tight, and it will keep two years. This gives the best flavour of the mushrooms to any sauce. If you put to a pint of this catchup a pint of mum, it will taste like foreign catchup.

RULES FOR BREWING.

Care must be taken to have clean malt; and after it is ground, it ought to stand four or five days.

For strong October, five quarters of malt to three hogsheads, and twenty-four pounds of hops. This

will afterwards make two hogsheads of good keeping small beer, allowing five pounds of hops to it.

For middling beer, a quarter of malt makes
a hogshead of ale, and one of small beer; or it
will make three hogsheads of good small beer,
allowing eight pounds of hops. This will keep all
the year: or it will make twenty gallons of strong
ale, and two hogsheads of small beer, that will
keep all the year.

If you intend to keep ale a great while, allow
a pound of hops to every bushel; if for six months,
five pounds to a hogshead; if for present drinking,
three pounds to a hogshead, and the softest and
clearest water you can get.

Observe the day before to have your vessels
clean, and never use your tubs for any other use,
except to make wines.

Let the casks be made clean the day before
with boiling water; and if the bung is big enough,
scrub them well with a little birch-broom or brush;
if they are very bad, take out the heads, and let
them be scrubbed clean with a hand-brush, sand,
and fuller's earth. Put on the heads again, and
scald them well, throw in the barrel a piece of un-
slacked lime, and stop the bung close.

The first copper of water, when it boils, pour in
the mash-tub, and let it be cool enough to see
your face in; then put in the malt, and let it be
well mashed; have a copper of water boiling in
the mean time, and when the malt is well mashed,
fill the mashing-tub, stir it well again, and cover it
over with the sacks. Let it stand three hours, set
a broad shallow tub under the cock, let it run
softly, and if it is thick throw it up again till it runs

fine, throw a handful of hops in the under tub, let
the mash run in it, and fill the tubs till all is run off.
Have water boiling in the copper, and lay as much
more on as you have occasion for, allowing one-
third for boiling and waste. Let it stand an hour,
boiling more water to fill the mash-tub for small
beer; let the fire down a little, and put it in tubs
enough to fill the mash. Let the second mash be
run off, and fill the copper with the first wort;
put in part of the hops, and boil it quick; an
hour is long enough; when it is half boiled, throw
in a handful of salt. Have a clean white wand,
and dip it in the copper, if the wort feels clammy,
it is boiled enough; slacken the fire, and take off
the wort. Have ready a large tub, put two sticks
across, and set the straining basket over the tub
on the sticks, and strain the wort through it. Put
the other wort on to boil with the rest of the hops;
let the mash be covered again with water, and
thin the wort that is cooled in as many things as
you can; for the thinner it lies, and the quicker it
cools, the better. When quite cool, put it in the
tunning tub. Throw a handful of salt in every
boil. When the mash has stood an hour, draw it
off, then fill the mash with cold water, take off
the wort in the copper, and order it as before.
When cool, add to it the first in the tub; as soon
as one copper is empty, fill the other, so boil small
beer well. Run off the last mash, and when both
are boiled with fresh hops, order them as the two
first boilings; when cool, empty the mash-tub, and
work the small beer there. When cool enough,
work it; set a wooden bowl full of yeast in the
beer, and it will work over with a little of the beer
in the boil. Stir the tun up every twelve hours,

let it stand two days, then tun it, taking off the yeast. Fill the vessels full, saving some to fill the barrels: let it stand till done working; lay on the bung lightly for a fortnight, after that stop it as close as you can. Mind you have a vent-peg at the top of the vessel; in warm weather open it; and if it hisses, loosen it till it has done, then stop it close again. If you can boil the ale at one boiling, it is best, if your copper will allow of it; if not, boil it as conveniency serves. When you draw the beer, and find it is not fine, draw off a gallon, and set it on the fire, with two ounces of isinglass, cut small and beat. Dissolve it in the beer over the fire; when it is all melted, let it stand till it is cold, and pour it in at the bung, which must lay loose on till it has done fermenting, then stop it close for a month.

Take care the casks are not musty, or have any ill taste; if they have, it is a hard thing to sweeten them.

You must wash the casks with cold water before you scald them, and they should lay a day or two soaking, and clean them well, then scald them.

When Beer has turned Sour.—To a kilderkin, put in at the bung a quart of oatmeal, lay the bung on loose two or three days, stop it down close, and let it stand a month. Some throw in a piece of chalk as big as a turkey's egg, and when it has done working, stop close for a month, then tap it.

OBSERVATIONS ON DISTILLING.

If your still be limbec, when you set it on fill the top with cold water, and make a little paste of flour and water, and close the bottom of your still well with it, and take great care that your fire

is not too hot to make it boil over, for that will
weaken the strength of your water; you must
change the water on the top of your still often,
and never let it be scalding hot, and your still will
drop gradually off; if you use a hot still, when you
put on the top dip a cloth in white lead and oil,
and lay it well over the edges of your still, and a
coarse wet cloth over the top : it requires a little
fire under it, but you must take care that you keep
it very clear ; when your cloth is dry, dip it in cold
water and lay it on again; and if your still be
hot, wet another cloth and lay it round the top,
and keep it of a moderate heat, so that your water
is cold when it comes off the still. If you use a
worm-still, keep your water in the tub full to the
top. and change the water often, to prevent it from
growing hot; observe to let all simple waters stand
two or three days before you work it, to take off
the fiery taste of the still.

TO DISTIL PEPPERMINT WATER.

Get your peppermint when it is full grown, and
before it seeds ; cut it in short lengths; fill your
still with it, and put it half full of water : then
make a good fire under it, and when it is nigh boiling, and the still begins to drop, if your fire be too
hot, draw a little out from under it, as you see it
requires, to keep it from boiling over, or your water
will be muddy ; the slower your still drops, the
water will be clearer and stronger, but do not
send it too far ; the next day bottle it, and let it
stand three or four days, to take off the fire of the
still ; then cork it well, and it will keep a long time.

TO DISTIL ELDER-FLOWERS.

Get your elder-flowers when they are in full bloom,

shake the blossoms off, and to every peck of flow-
ers put one quart of water, and let them steep in it
all night; then put them in a cold still, and take
care that your water comes cold off the still, and
it will be very clear, and draw it no longer than
your liquor is good; then put it into bottles, and
cork it in two or three days, and it will keep
a year.

TO DISTIL ROSE WATER.

Gather your red roses when they are dry and
full blown; pick off the leaves, and to every peck
put one quart of water; then put them into a cold
still, and make a slow fire under it; the slower you
distil it, the better it is; then bottle it, and cork it
in two or three days time, and keep it for use.——
N.B. You distil bean-flowers the same way.

TO DISTIL PENNY-ROYAL WATER.

Get your penny-royal when it is full grown, and
before it is in blossom, then fill your cold still with
it, and put it half full of water; make a moderate
fire under it, and distil it off cold; then put it into
bottles, and cork it in two or three days time, and
keep it for use.

TO DISTIL LAVENDER WATER.

To every twelve pounds of lavender-neps put
one quart of water; put them into a cold still, and
make a slow fire under it, and distil it off very
slow, and put it into a pot till you have distilled it
off as slow as before; then put it into bottles, and
cork it well.

TO DISTIL SPIRITS OF WINE.

Take the bottoms of strong beer, and any kind
of wines; put them into a hot still about three
parts full; then make a very slow fire under, and

if you do not take great care to keep it moderate, it will boil over, for the body is so strong that it will rise to the top of the still; the slower you distil it, the stronger your spirit will be; put it into an earthen pot till you have done distilling, then clean your still well out, and, put the spirit into it, and distil it slow as before, and make it as strong as to burn in your lamp; then bottle it and cork it well, and keep it for use.

DIRECTIONS FOR MAKING BLANC MANGE.

Put one ounce and a half of isinglass into a stew-pan to boil, with about half a pint of water, put it to the side of the stove so as to barely simmer; when dissolved, strain it into another stew-pan, that has a pint of good cream, a pint of good milk, the peel of a lemon, and a little cinnamon and sugar in it: blanch three ounces of sweet almonds, and half an ounce of bitter; then put them in the mortar, and pound them very fine, put a spoonful of water to them several times while pounding, as it keeps them white; when sufficiently fine to go through the tammy, put them to the milk and cream: put the stew-pan on the fire to boil for about fifteen minutes, then rub it through the tammy; be sure and get all the almonds through; when half cold put in about a gill of ratafia, if convenient, otherwise a glass of brandy: when it begins to get thick put it in the mould.

BEST SORT OF PLUMB PUDDING.

One pound of raisins stoned; one pound of currants, well washed and picked; a pound of suet, chopped very fine; about a pound of flour, and as many bread-crumbs; a little fine spice, and an ounce of preserved lemon-peel; the same quantity of orange-peel and citron; about half a nutmeg, grated; and a quarter of a pound of moist sugar; mix all well together; then break in seven eggs, stir it well up, add about a quarter of a pint of milk, and a gill of brandy; mix all well together; if it should want a little more milk, put it in, but be careful that you do not wet it much; let it be stiff enough for the spoon to stand upright, otherwise the fruit will settle at the bottom, which will spoil the look of it; it will take four hours to boil.

RECIPES FOR THE SICK.

WHITE WINE WHEY.

Boil half a pint of new milk; as soon as it boils up, pour in a glass of white wine; boil it up, and set the saucepan aside till the curd subsides. Pour the whey off, and add to it half a pint of boiling water, and a bit of white sugar. Whey may be made of vinegar, and diluted with boiling water and sugar. It is less heating than wine, and if to excite perspiration, answers as well.

ARTIFICIAL ASSES MILK.

Boil a quart of new milk, with a quart of water, an ounce of white sugar-candy, half an ounce of eringo roots, and half an ounce of conserve of roses, till reduced to half. The doses must be regulated by the effect.

BALM TEA.

Take a quantity of fresh gathered balm-leaves, put them into a stone jar, and pour boiling water over them : cover the jar with a linen cloth, three or four times doubled, to keep in the steam, and let it stand till cold. This is a very refreshing drink in fevers, &c.

A CLEAR BROTH TO KEEP.

Put the mouse-buttock of beef, a knuckle of veal, and some mutton shanks, into a pan, just cover with water; put a paste over it; when the beef is tender, it is done. Cover it up close, and keep it in a cool place.

MUTTON BROTH.

Take a loin of mutton, cut off the fat, put to it one quart of water, boil and skim it well; put in a piece of upper crust of bread, a blade of mace, and boil it slowly an hour; pour the broth clean off; season with salt, and the mutton will be fit to eat. Turnips must be boiled by themselves in another saucepan.

BEEF TEA.

Cut a pound of lean beef fine. Pour a pint of boiling water over to raise the scum, skin, strain, and let it settle; pour it clear off, and it will be fit for use.

CALF'S FEET BROTH.

Boil two calf's feet with two ounces of veal, two of beef, a piece of crust, two or three blades of mace, half a nutmeg sliced, and salt, in three quarts of water, till reduced to half; strain, and take off the fat.

EEL BROTH.

Clean half a pound of eels, set them on the fire with a quart of water, an onion, and a few peppercorns: simmer till the eels are broken, and the broth good.

TAPIOCA JELLY.

Wash tapioca in several waters. Soak it in fresh water five hours, and simmer in the same till quite clear. Add lemon-juice, wine, and sugar.

CHICKEN PANADA.

Boil a chicken, till three parts done, in a quart of·

water, take off the skim, cut the white meat off, and pound it in a mortar to a paste, with a little of the water it was boiled in; season with salt, nutmeg, and a little lemon-peel. Boil it gently for a few minutes. It should be tolerably thick.

PANADA.

Put a little water in a saucepan, with a glass of wine, sugar, nutmeg, and lemon-peel. When it boils, put some grated bread in, and boil it fast. When of a proper thickness to drink, take it off. It is very good with a little rum and butter, instead of the wine.

EGGS.

An egg broken into a cup of tea, or beaten up and mixed with a basin of milk, makes a very nutritious breakfast.

An egg divided, and the yolk and the white beaten separately, then mixed with a glass of wine, will afford two very wholesome draughts, and be much better than when taken together.

Beat up a new-laid egg, and mix it with a quarter of a pint of new milk warmed, a spoonful of capillaire, one of rose water, and a little nutmeg. It should not be warmed after the egg is put in. Take it the first and last thing.

ARROW ROOT.

Mixed with milk, and sweetened, is very nutritious.

ISINGLASS.

Boil an ounce of isinglass-shavings with forty peppercorns, and a crust of bread, in a quart of water, simmer to a pint, and strain it off.

This will keep well, and may be taken in wine and water, milk, tea, soup, or whatever may be preferred.

WHITE POT.

Beat up eight eggs, (leave out half the whites) with a pint of milk, a little rose water, nutmeg, and a quarter of a pound of sugar. Cut a roll into thin slices, and pour the milk and eggs over them. Put a piece of butter ou the top, and bake it for half an hour.

WATER GRUEL.

Put a pint of water on the fire. Mix in a bason a large spoonful of oatmeal with a little water; when the water boils, stir in the oatmeal, and let it boil up three or four times. Strain it through a sieve, put in salt, and a piece of butter. Stir it till the butter is melted, and it will be fine and smooth. Sugar, or a spoonful of wine, may be added.

BARLEY WATER.

Put a quarter of a pound of pearl-barley to two quarts of water. Boil it half away, and strain it off. Add two spoonsful of white wine, and sweeten to taste.

CAUDLE.

Make gruel of grots; when well boiled, stir it till cold. Add sugar, wine, brandy, and nutmeg.

RICH CAUDLE.

Pour into boiling water, grated rice, mixed with a little cold water; when of a proper consistence, add sugar, cinnamon, and a glass of brandy. Boil all together.

BROWN CAUDLE.

Make a gruel with six spoonsful of oatmeal. Add a quart of malt liquor, not bitter; boil, sweeten, and add half a pint of white wine, with spices, or not.

SAGO.

Soak it in cold water one hour, pour it off, wash it; add water, and simmer till the sago is clear, with spice, if approved.   Add wine and sugar, and boil all up together.

GROUND RICE MILK.

Put a spoonful of ground rice to three pints of milk, add cinnamon and nutmeg.   Sweeten to your taste.

MUSTARD WHEY.

Turn half a pint of boiling milk with a table-spoonful of made mustard.   Strain the whey from the curd, and drink it in bed.   This will give a glowing warmth.

This has been known to be very efficacious in nervous affections, as well as the palsy.

A VERY REFRESHING DRINK.

Pour a table-spoonful of capillaire, and one of vinegar, into a tumbler of cold spring water.

BUTTER MILK.

Milk a cow into a small churn; when it has stood about ten minutes begin churning, and con-tinue till the flakes of butter swim about thick, and the milk appears thin and blue.   Drink of it very frequently.

The food should be biscuits and rusks; ripe and dried fruits of various kinds, where a decline is apprehended.

ALE POSSET.

Put a small piece of bread into a pint of milk, and set it over the fire.   Put nutmeg and sugar into a pint of ale, and when your milk boils, pour it upon the ale.   Let it stand a few minutes to clear, and it will be fit for use.

THE END.

J. Evans, Printer, 91, Bartholomew Close.

CPSIA information can be obtained
at www.ICGtesting.com
Printed in the USA
LVHW031600130522
718729LV00012B/715